Happy Me, Happy You

Happy Me, Happy You

The Huna Way to Healthy Relationships

SERGE KAHILI KING

QUEST
BOOKS

Theosophical Publishing House
Wheaton, Illinois * Chennai, India

Quest Books
Theosophical Publishing House
PO Box 270
Wheaton, IL 60187-0270

www.questbooks.net

Cover design by Drew Stevens
Typesetting by DataPage, Inc.

Library of Congress Cataloging-in-Publication Data

King, Serge.
Happy me, happy you: the Huna way to healthy relationships / Serge
Kahili King.
pages   cm
Originally published: Volcano, Hawaii: Hunaworks, 2006.
Includes index.
ISBN 978-0-8356-0920-3
1. Self-actualization (Psychology).   2. Interpersonal relations.
3. Huna.   4. Shamanism—Hawaii.   I. Title.
BF637.S4K54846 2014
299'.9242—dc23   2013039924

5   4   3   2   1   *   14   15   16   17   18   19   20

Printed in the United States of America

Contents

Acknowledgments

I would like to acknowledge and give thanks to all those who helped me to write this book, including my parents, Harry and Joyce; my great-grandparents and grandparents; my brothers, Harry, Loring, and Darrel; my sisters, Dee and Marilyn; my awesome wife, Gloria; our children, Chris, Pierre, and Dion; my extended family of relatives that includes aunts and uncles and cousins, nieces and nephews, in-laws and grandchildren; my Hawaiian family and my Aloha International ohana; my students and friends all over the world; and even those few who have decided that they don't like me at all. Thank you all for being my teachers.

Part 1

THE FUNDAMENTALS

Chapter 1

Relationship Basics

In old Hawaii there were many legends of how things came to be. Here is one from the Kahili family of Kauai:

In a time before time, in a place where there were no places, there was *Kumulipo*, the deep, dark, profound, and mysterious void. In that infinite emptiness was an infinite potential, waiting to be filled but unable to manifest because of the tension between two forces: *Wakea*, the male force of Chaos, and *Papa*, the female force of Order.

At some timeless point the tension gave way. Chaotic movement interacted with Order's stillness to form the First Wave. Out of that First Wave was manifested the First Relationship. And there's been Trouble ever since.

WHY PEOPLE RELATE

Waves exist because of a relationship between movement and stillness, and everything exists in a multitude of relationships with other things. Not all relationships are healthy, however, in terms of being beneficial to whomever or whatever is related. This is especially true of human relationships. Considering all the differences between men and women, men and men, women and women, cultures and environments, and everything else, it is a mystery and a wonder that anyone ever gets along with anyone.

And yet, they do. Most people, most of the time, do get along; lots of people, some of the time, don't; and a few people all of the time never do. This book is primarily for the second group.

What is amazing is that so many people figure out how to get along all by themselves, without any help. What's sad is that so many people don't know how to do it, for whatever reason. Aside from those who just don't want to get along with others, I think that everyone who *does* want to can do so. I also think that all it takes is some simple knowledge of what to do and how to do it.

If we want to understand relationships, we have to understand why people want to relate in the first place. People don't do anything without a good reason, especially something as difficult as establishing and maintaining a good relationship with someone else. So what kind of reason could be compelling enough for people to undertake something as difficult as relating to another human being?

The answer lies in what motivates people to do anything at all, from getting up in the morning, to relating and working and playing during the day, to going to bed at night. All human behavior is rooted in something so fundamental that it is usually overlooked. I am reminded of an old joke about a man who is standing on a street corner, hitting himself on the head with a hammer. When a passerby asks him why he is doing that, he says, "Because it feels so good when I stop."

Everybody, really, just wants to feel good. It's as simple as that. People get up in the morning when it feels better than lying in bed. People go to work when work itself, or some benefit provided by work (like food, shelter, or clothing), makes them feel better than they would without it. People play games when such play makes them feel good, or when playing gives them something else that makes them feel good, like money, health, or praise. People go to bed at night when that makes them feel better than not going to bed. And people relate to other people—putting up with all kinds of inconveniences, difficulties, and dangers in order to do so— when relating makes them feel better than not relating.

That's all well and good, you may say, but it seems too general to be useful. You are right, so let's look more closely at what makes people feel good.

What Is "Feeling Good"?

Before discussing what makes people feel good, we ought to examine what "feeling good" really means. Basically, it is a physiological sensation of pleasure. Even when you feel good because you've solved a problem in arithmetic (or algebra, or geometry, or calculus, or a crossword puzzle, etc.), there is a physiological response that we interpret as pleasure. Like it or not, the body is always involved in any experience of feeling good, whether we associate the experience with our body, our mind, or our spirit.

The actual sensation of feeling good comes from a sudden release of physical tension. A small release of tension produces a small sensation of pleasure, and a large release of tension produces a large sensation of pleasure. Sometimes, however, a sudden release of tension produces a sudden *increase* of tension, which we call fear or anger, but otherwise a release of tension generally just feels good. As to what causes the sudden release of tension, one common element in many experiences is sudden change. I remember reading a US marketing report stating that retailers could generally count on a significant increase in shoppers right after any change in the weather. According to the report, it didn't matter whether the weather changed from sunny to rainy or rainy to sunny. In either case the number of shoppers would increase. The sudden change in weather released tension in people, which led to increased activity.

One source of pleasure a relationship produces has to do with the amount and frequency of tension release it provides. Sexual activity will immediately come to mind for many people, but that is only one of many opportunities for tension release, and therefore for feeling good, in relationships.

Another common element in many pleasurable experiences involving the sudden release of tension is based on the engagement of familiar patterns. There is an old saying in English that "familiarity breeds contempt," meaning that the more familiar something or someone is, the less importance and respect it receives. However, this is only valid when the familiar thing or person stimulates resistance, i.e., tension. Much more often, "familiarity breeds pleasure." Thus the pleasure we derive from hobbies, holidays, games the rules of which we know well, playing music, dancing, and—when there is no reason for resistance—encounters with beloved family members and old friends. Experiencing familiar people, places, things, and habits provides a sense of security, accompanied by a release of tension, and that feels good.

DIFFERENCES AND SIMILARITIES

Someone sent me an anonymous quote that I like a lot: "Men are from Earth, women are from Earth. Deal with it."

It may be useful and amusing to look at the differences between men and women in how they behave and think. Some differences are due to physiology, of course, but most of them are due to culture. However, many differences that are valid in one society may not apply at all in another one.

There is a famous legend in Hawaii about Pele, the volcano goddess, and her younger sister, Hi'iaka. In this story, Pele is the unquestioned leader of a mostly female group. She has no male counterpart, no male with any authority over her, but she does have numerous lovers (not uncommon among female chiefs in Hawaiian society). One of these is Lohiau, a chief of Kauai. As the story goes, Pele is on the Big Island of Hawaii and wants her younger sister to go to Kauai and fetch Lohiau for her. As part of the deal, in a translation by Nathaniel Emerson, Pele says that after Hi'iaka brings Lohiau back, "For five nights and five days he shall be mine; after that, the taboo shall be off and he shall be yours." This doesn't exactly fit the Western stereotype, but it does reflect important aspects of Hawaiian culture and the importance of cultural differences in human behavior.

My contention, then, is that most perceived differences between male and female behavior are culturally derived. In teaching men and women around the world about relationships and how to improve them, I use the same concepts and techniques for both genders and get the same results, because the similarities between them transcend the differences.

LOVE, POWER, AND HARMONY

With the above said, we can get on with the three primary motivators for feeling good that all human beings share. There is no need to make up any fancy names. Human beings, male and female, are all motivated either by love, or by power, or by harmony, or by various combinations of all three at the same time. Once you understand how this works, it becomes simple to understand any sort of human behavior at all, including your own.

The Urge to Love and Be Loved

As a motivation, love is the urge to connect with someone or something. Humans are not very particular about what it is they connect with, which is why we can love not only people, but places, animals, plants, things (this covers a huge range of possibilities), and ideas, plus any other category I haven't thought to mention.

In any situation where fear and anger are absent, or at least weaker than the urge to connect, human beings will fall in love with each other. Cultural and personal preferences will determine whether they become lovers or friends, but they will inevitably connect. This is the reason for the so-called "bonding" effect between individuals and within groups of any kind.

Love is part of our nature. It is the state of feeling happily connected to someone else or the act of becoming connected. It is extending our self to include another. We do not have to strive for love unless we feel we do not have it. When human beings gather under circumstances where there is no fear, love simply happens. I have attended many gatherings in many different countries where dozens of complete strangers became loving friends after two or three days of just being together. What they did and why they were there didn't seem to matter. Merely close proximity and a lack of fear produced love without effort.

In times of danger, love also manifests naturally. When there is a disaster or an accident, people who are not incapacitated by fear automatically begin to assist the ones who need help. They don't have to be taught or instructed, except in how to help better. The desire to help, which is a form of love, arises spontaneously. This automatic love response is so great that some people will put their own lives at great risk to help another person, even a complete stranger. We call such people heroes when they jump into raging rivers to save someone from drowning, or run into a burning building to bring out a child, or do any one of a hundred other brave things to help another. And yet, few of such people think of themselves as heroes. Most of the time, they say they acted because it was the thing to do, or they did it without thinking. It was a spontaneous act of love.

Doubt is the one thing that weakens the connection of love. When a person doubts the existence of love, fear is born and love begins to die. Fear and love are in opposition. Fear comes from feeling or being disconnected. When love diminishes, fear increases; and when fear diminishes, love increases. Moreover, when love diminishes, so does the need and desire for love.

The need and desire to love and be loved influence all our actions and reactions. To the degree that we feel a lack of love in any form, some form of fear will accompany that need and desire. In addition to the powerful force of sexual love, we are also driven by a love for approval and recognition. Many of our behaviors are guided by the hope of approval or in reaction to disapproval. And many are guided by a quest for recognition, however small or temporary, especially when affection and approval do not seem imminent. Ironically, great acts that benefit all of society and vicious acts that do equal harm may both come from the need and desire for recognition. When recognition is lacking, some people will force it by seeking respect, perhaps through doing something worthwhile, or perhaps through achieving a false respect by causing fear.

When the attempt to satisfy the need and desire for love of any kind is sufficiently frustrated, the result is mental, emotional, or physical behavior that tends to disrupt relationships. This happens when the fear that results from the lack of love has no outlet. When, according to the individual's beliefs, nothing can be done, the fear causes a withdrawal inward, producing great tension in the body and therefore a greater and greater disconnection from others.

The Urge to Empower and Be Empowered

Power is part of our nature, too. As with love, we do not have to strive for power unless we feel we do not have it. Power itself is the act of being effective. From the very moment of conception we are all in the process of expressing our power, of doing—or of trying to do—that which is effective for our survival and our pleasure.

Physically, our bodies are constantly engaged in maintenance, repair, growth, learning, and pleasure seeking. Mentally, our minds are constantly engaged in problem solving, creativity, and extending our influence into the world around us. We are always powerful, but for many reasons we may not always realize it. When the expression of power is not effective, or we do not *believe* it to be effective, the natural reaction is to seek a different solution to a problem or to find another way of being effective.

Inventors may experiment with thousands of different approaches before their inventions work; sports teams may try dozens of different strategies to win against their opponents; politicians may devise many different economic and social plans to achieve their ends. Individually, people try different healing techniques and approaches, different

11

careers, different relationships, and different religions with the aim of being more effective in their lives.

Again, doubt is the one thing that weakens the natural expression of power. When a person doubts his or her personal power, or source of power, then anger is born and power begins to flee. As power decreases, anger increases, and as anger decreases, power increases. And, as is true regarding love, when power decreases, so does the need and desire for power.

The most popular technique for trying to regain power while doubt and anger are still operating is the control approach. Many people confuse power with control, but actually, control is what people use when they feel powerless. When we use *active* control to force people to do what we want, it is usually in the form of intimidation or physical force. On the other hand, when we use *passive* control—also called passive aggression—we try to get people to do what we want by refusing to act or by making them feel guilty. Besides being bad for relationships and effectiveness, the attempt to control causes a lot of tension in the controller.

When control isn't possible, another technique sometimes used is vandalism. A child who feels hurt and powerless may break things to display anger. This seldom works to control parents, but it does get a reaction, and that brings a little satisfaction, at least. The child thinks, "I can't get what I want, but at least I can make someone unhappy." It is a poor substitute for effectiveness, but it can progress from childhood tantrums to teenage vandalism to adult terrorism. And of course it brings tension with it.

However, when there is no outlet for the anger and no return to real power, the person directs the anger inward, and the result is mental, emotional, and physical resistance to almost all other human behavior.

The Urge to Harmonize

Finally, human beings have a natural inclination toward harmony. By harmony, I mean the mutually beneficial integration and cooperation of people with their social and natural environment. We can see this behavior most easily in isolated tribal groups, but it exists also in many small communities, neighborhoods, groups, clubs, and associations.

We may see attempts to create harmony by national governments and the United Nations, but the larger the group, the more difficult success seems to be. This is partly because the larger the group, the easier it is for it to be more impersonal. That is, the easier it is to lose a sense of personal connection and influence.

But harmony involves more than a sense of personal connection. It really has to do with a broader sense of one's place and purpose in the world and of one's interdependence with it. When a person doubts such interdependence and her own place and purpose within it, then alienation is born. Instead of "you and I" or "we and they" together, it becomes "me or us against them." Alienation, which often includes extreme confusion, restlessness, apathy, and despair, creates great internal tension and, of course, mental, emotional, and physical disharmony.

The solution for relationship problems caused by fear is to be more loving by giving more mercy, acknowledgment, appreciation, admiration, tolerance, caring, and help to others and to yourself. The solution for relationship problems caused by anger is to increase your knowledge, skill, and self-confidence. The solution for relationship problems caused by alienation is first to seek spiritual harmony with a higher or deeper being and then to look for that spirit in all things. If you want a quick fix, though, because of the ultra-fast pace of modern life, then simply cease to doubt. Keep a healthy skepticism whenever necessary, but refuse to doubt your own value, the value of others, and the value of the world. If that solution sounds too simple, keep reading.

THE RULES WE LIVE BY

Many people spend their entire lives seeking to know the laws or rules of the universe, so I've decided to save them a lot of time by giving those rules out now, for free. Be fore-warned that these concepts are based on a shamanic view in which everything is alive, aware, and responsive.

The universe and everything in it has three aspects: Spirit, Body, and Mind. Each of these aspects has its own rules. The better we understand these rules the easier it will be for us to grow, to heal, and to have a good time.

Spirit has one rule only: "experience existence." That's it. No conditions, no shoulds, no limits. And no avoiding it.

The Body only has two rules: "seek pleasure" and "avoid pain." Since the way to do this is not always clear under all circumstances, the Body will sometimes move toward pain in order to experience some associated sensory or emotional pleasure—as in climbing a mountain for the pleasure of the view, working out for the energy benefit, or undergoing surgery to get well. Sometimes pleasure does not seem to be an option, in which case the Body will try to move toward the least pain. We can see this behavior in people who drink themselves sick to suppress emotional pain, or who stay in bad relationships for fear of having none at all, or who commit violent suicide. Then there are those who move away from pleasure for fear of an associated pain, such as people who avoid success for fear of criticism, those who believe that pleasure is a sin punishable by God, and those who believe that pleasure makes you weak. For the most part, however, it is easy to note that all spontaneous, intuitive, and subconscious behavior follows the simple rule of seeking pleasure and avoiding pain.

What about the Mind? Hooboy! The Mind is a rule-making fanatic. It makes rules—lots and lots of rules—about everything imaginable. It makes rules about language, rules about religion, rules about behavior, even rules about the Universe. And when it wants something badly enough, why, it goes right ahead and changes the rules. So we have hundreds of languages around the world, hundreds of cultures based on their own ideas of right and wrong, hundreds of ways to relate to God, hundreds of scientific theories about hundreds of subjects, hundreds of countries with their own variations on political systems, hundreds of thousands of laws governing behavior in different societies . . . you get the idea. Ask anyone's opinion about anything, and what you will hear are the rules they live by. They may call their rules opinions, beliefs, or facts, but they are all rules, some inherited, some borrowed, and some made up.

Breaking rules is tricky. Just try to break the rule of Spirit. Nonexistence does not seem to be an option. And when you try to break the rules of the Body you usually get severe and immediate physical or emotional consequences. The Body wants its pleasure and fears all pain, so woe to the Mind that tries to alter these natural inclinations without good reason.

There are consequences to breaking the rules of the Mind, but they depend on which rules are involved and who else is involved with them. You can break a legal law with impunity if no one else is around, unless you confuse legality with morality (they do coincide, occasionally). If you break a moral law, one that you've accepted as your own, when no one else is around, you'll probably punish yourself. You can break the rules of language, but you risk being misunderstood. You can break the rules of science anytime you want, as long as you are not seeking a grant, but some things may not work the way you want them to. You can break the social rules of your group, if you don't mind being cast out.

I don't recommend breaking rules. I recommend using the rules of Spirit and the Body and playing creatively with the rules and rule-making talent of the Mind. Regarding the Mind, it's much easier to make different rules than to try to break old ones. Rules that are not used any longer just fade away. People make up rules all the time. You can make different rules about how you think and how you feel, about what is possible and what you can do, and about what the past means and what the future will bring. The rules you use affect your behavior and your experience. Change your rules and your life will change. This book will help you to examine the rules that you use for relationships and to create new ones if you want to.

What This Book Is About

This is a book about healing relationships. At the same time, it is not about healing relationships at all. No, I am not trying to confuse you. Rather, I am trying to help you understand more clearly what relationships really are. Many people today are reading, writing, teaching, and complaining about relationships. Nevertheless, too many relationships don't seem to get better. In my counseling work I hear a lot of comments from clients like the following: "My relationship just isn't working." "My partner doesn't want to discuss our relationship." "I've tried everything I know to make this relationship work." "I've decided not to have another relationship." The examples could go on and on, but these will suffice because the problem is obvious.

Isn't it? If not, then let me make it obvious. The problem is that too many people spend more time on improving the relationship than they do on improving how they relate. When that happens, instead of a couple they become a group, with the relationship as an entity practically taking on a life of its own. While I do believe that everything is alive, aware, and responsive, I also know that when people work on "the relationship" instead of on themselves, they are merely distracting themselves from the real problem. That is because, as alive as it might be in some esoteric sense, a "relationship" is no more than an abstract, intellectual concept—a *thought form*, if you prefer—and bears no resemblance to a living, breathing, human being.

Relationships don't think in any human way. They don't act; they don't change anything. There is really no such thing as a "relationship" in the sense of something that exists apart from people who relate. My "relationship" with my wife is not a thing. It is merely a word for the way we relate. We can completely ignore our *relationship* and get along just fine. We cannot, though, ignore the way we *relate* to each other and continue to get along fine.

Hence, the problem between two people is never a "relationship" that isn't working. It is always that one or both of them don't know how to relate to the other in a better way. So the problem is actually behavioral, and it's a lot easier to change behavior than it is to change an abstract concept called "a relationship." When two people communicate thoughtfully and take care to respond to each other's behavior, they create a good relationship automatically in the way they relate.

Is this just another book on behavior modification, then? Well, yes and no. It is a book on how to change your behavior in order to create healthier relationships with other people and the world around you. But my ideas on the best methods for doing that are a bit out of the ordinary because of my background in alternative and complementary healing. For instance, I am going to show you how to examine physical, emotional, mental, and energetic behavior in your various relationships, and I am going to show you how to improve those relationships using objective, subjective, symbolic, and holistic techniques.

EXAMINING BEHAVIOR

Physical behavior includes how you relate to your own body, because that influences how others will relate to you. It also includes how you move and use your body as you relate to others.

Emotional behavior has to do with your feelings about yourself and others, including how you express emotions and how you suppress them. Whether you know it or not, or even whether you believe it or not, other people can be affected subtly or dramatically by the way you feel.

Mental behavior involves everything from the words you speak to the words you think, as well as the memories, fantasies, and expectations you dwell on. These also affect people much more than you might realize, and I will explain how.

Energetic behavior is based on the idea that you are more than just a bag of bones, meat, and blood, and that the energy you radiate or project, consciously or subconsciously, affects other people, too.

CHAPTER 1

TYPES OF TECHNIQUES

Objective techniques include changes that you can make in your posture, your breathing, your movements, your physical actions and reactions, and your speech patterns.

Subjective techniques are based on an assumption that telepathy is one of our natural forms of communication; these techniques include ways of modifying your thoughts and feelings.

Symbolic techniques are based on shamanic healing ideas involving self-guided imagery to help improve relationships.

Holistic techniques include role modeling to develop patterns of behavior that might be more useful to you than the ones you've been using.

HOW THIS BOOK IS ORGANIZED

In order to help the greatest number of people with the greatest number of relationship problems, I have divided this book into three parts.

Part 1 is about fundamental concepts and practices that affect all relationships. In addition to chapter 1 on relationship basics, there are chapters on criticism and praise and on forgiveness.

Part 2 is about learning how to relate better to yourself, because this is your primary relationship and its state will affect all your other relationships. First, there will be a chapter on relating to your own body, then one on relating to your own mind, and then one on relating to your own spirit.

Part 3 deals directly with your relationships to other people. The first chapter in this part is about relating to your family. Next is a chapter on friends and friendship, followed by one on relationships with lovers and spouses and then by a chapter on relationships with other kinds of people.

Every chapter contains ideas and techniques that you can use with a little modification in any relationship. As many of my readers know, my teachings are based on a Hawaiian philosophy of life called Huna, which is expressed in my family tradition as a set of seven principles or ideas about life that can be applied to any endeavor or area of life. Here are those principles as they concern relationships:

1. The world is what you think it is, and therefore, the state, quality, or nature of a relationship is defined by you.

2. There are no limits, and you are free to change your mind about any relationship, or redefine it in any way you choose in order to change your experience of it.

3. Energy flows where attention goes, and whatever part of a relationship to which you give most of your attention is the part most energized, for good or ill.

4. Now is the moment of power, and it is in the present moment that relationships are healed, or not.

5. To love is to be happy with someone, and the more things you like about the person to whom you are relating, the healthier and happier the relationship will be.

6. All power comes from within, and you are the one who chooses how to relate.

7. Effectiveness is the measure of truth, and if one plan for healing a relationship doesn't work, you can always make a new plan if you want to.

Although this book has plenty of ideas and techniques for helping you relate well, it does not attempt to cover all types and degrees of relationships. That would require a much bigger book. My main hope is that you will find it useful.

Eia ke känaenae a ka mea hele: he leo, he leo wale no.
This is the offering of a traveler: advice, only advice.

Chapter 2

Criticism and Praise

The only way to influence someone's behavior is to do something that motivates them to act in the way you want them to. I've already mentioned the motivations of love, power, and harmony. They are effective when used properly, but, unfortunately, too few people have experience in doing that. What more people are experienced in is how to use the negative motivation of fear.

One primary kind of fear used to motivate people is that of physical harm. Many parents apply physical punishment, or the threat of it, as a means of controlling their children. My own father had a great big leather strap, the kind that barbers used to use for sharpening straight razors. He never actually used it on me, because his simply opening the drawer where he kept the strap was enough to get me to change my behavior immediately. When I drove my mother into a frenzy, she would whack my behind with a wooden hanger, and that motivated me for a while.

Using the fear of physical punishment to motivate people is very inefficient, however. For one thing, applying the punishment requires a lot of energy and attention.

For another thing, people become adept at avoiding punishment in various ways and can even build up a tolerance to it. Finally, punishment has a strong tendency to cause a great deal of suppressed anger and resentment, which can have many negative repercussions for the punishers.

Much more common, efficient, and devastating is the control of people's behavior through criticism. Fear of criticism is probably the single greatest fear human beings have; and, directly or indirectly, it has influenced the lives of all people on this planet. Some people may be free of this fear as adults, but it would be an extremely rare person who wasn't affected by it as a child. The power of criticism as a means of control comes from the fact that everyone, innately, wants to be loved, and everyone can be trained to believe that love can be withheld. It is this threat that produces the fear.

Now, what exactly is the threat here? It is the threat of annihilation. It is the threat of ceasing to exist, of not being nourished, of being abandoned. That is the nature of the experience when you, as a young child, are criticized. And what does the criticism engender? Terror! Because, from a child's point of view, these people you live with—these enormous giants—are your support, your source of life, your source of protection, and you can't make it without them. So any threat of abandonment by them is literally a matter of life and death. Unfortunately, as people grow older they seldom forget this early training. I worked with a woman in her sixties who had a very hard time turning down other people's requests for help, even when her health and finances were negatively effected. During a session involving deep focus, we had the following dialogue with her subconscious:

> Serge: "What would happen if you said no when people asked for your help?"
>
> Woman: "They wouldn't like me."
>
> Serge: "What would happen if they didn't like you?"
>
> Woman: "They would not want me to be around them."
>
> Serge: "And what would happen if they didn't want you around them?"
>
> Woman: "Then they would throw me out into the street and I would starve to death and I would die."

When the woman considered this dialogue consciously, she knew that it came from childhood memories and was obviously absurd in the present time. But it served to clarify the reason for her difficulty in refusing people, and she was able to use this knowledge to change her behavior. Whenever someone asked her to do something she didn't want to do or something she believed was not good for her, she reminded herself that no one was going to throw her out in the street to starve and die if she said no.

THE SUBTLE APPROACH TO CRITICISM

In some families, criticism of the children is so subtle that neither the child nor the parent may consciously recognize it as such. In the United States in the 1950s, when children asked where they came from they were still commonly told they had been brought by a stork. Some parents tell children they were found under a cabbage leaf, like some castaway object. Another popular comment, if the parent is upset with a child, is to say that the child is going to be given back to the Indians. Parents may say such things jokingly, and it's funny for them, but not for the child. The subtle message is that the child doesn't really belong to the family, and this can make a small child feel tremendously insecure and unloved and somehow "wrong" for the rest of his or her life. After a while the child sees the parents smile when they say such things, and the child learns to smile on the outside, but on the inside his or her stomach is churning. For an adult, when accompanied by a sufficient lack of familial affection plus a sufficient lack of self-confidence and self-esteem, this kind of memory can result in an inability to feel a strong connection with any group. In some cases, people may even feel alienated from the entire human race.

Another subtle type of criticism may occur when people think that they are encouraging someone to do better. Encouraging someone is a good thing, of course, unless there is no appreciation for accomplishment. When I was in elementary school, every time I came home with a report card, no matter how good it was my mother would always say, "You can do better." She thought she was spurring me on to greater endeavors, but the effect was for me to believe that nothing I did was ever good enough. Therefore I wasn't good enough, so why try hard? It was only after ending up next to the bottom in my high school class, failing spectacularly in my first year of college, and spending three years in the US Marine Corps that I got over that one.

A third form of subtle criticism takes place when nothing a person says or does is taken seriously. Often this is a kind of disempowerment technique. Older siblings may use it to keep a younger sibling subordinate, so-called friends may use it to maintain leadership control, and parents may use it to keep children from threatening the parental hierarchy. A friend told me how this dynamic played out in her house. Upon finally receiving a degree in Oriental Medicine, she went home to get some praise from her father, who immediately said, "Let's see what Uncle Jerry thinks. He had acupuncture once." This kind of criticism tends to increase one's sense of worthlessness if it isn't counteracted.

Finally, there is the destructively insidious kind of criticism that is never spoken aloud but conveyed by look, gesture, or other behavior. Often it is accompanied by telepathic thought, emotionally charged or not. Here, I'm not talking about a look or a gesture given to communicate that another person has broken a rule, as my wife does when she frowns and flutters her hand when she thinks I'm driving too close to the car in front of us. Instead, I'm talking about a look, gesture, movement, or thought that means, "I don't like you; I don't want you; I wish you would disappear." This kind of criticism takes its worst form when, outwardly, the subtle critic says and does things that indicate the opposite—like saying, "Of course I love you," while turning and looking away at the same time—which leaves the victim feeling not only confused, but unhappy and guilty for feeling that way.

CHAPTER 2

THE DIRECT APPROACH TO CRITICISM

Receiving direct criticism in response to doing something wrong is practically unavoidable for most people at some time or another; and while it might not be pleasant to hear, most people can handle it without serious problems, especially when it is deserved. What comes close to pure evil, in my opinion, is the constant barrage of criticism in the form of fault finding, condemnation, blaming, disapproval, and cursing that some people habitually inflict on others, especially parents in relation to their children. It doesn't matter if the purpose is to correct mistakes, to manipulate behavior, to vent frustration, or to hide one's own feelings of inadequacy; this kind of criticism is a terrible thing to do to a child at whatever age. Developing self-confidence and self-esteem in life is hard enough without running a gauntlet of daily criticism as well. I have nothing but the highest regard for people who have survived such a critical environment to become loving, helpful, friendly human beings, and I feel deep compassion for those who are still struggling with its effects.

Direct criticism is most often used for correcting someone's mistakes. Although popular worldwide, it is, in fact, an inefficient method for making corrections. The problem is that the act of criticizing produces tension in the critic as well as in the recipient. Too much tension interferes with memory and so affects learning and skills. During one of my courses, a woman was taking tennis lessons in her spare time. The tennis instructor used a critical approach until the student, using ideas from the course, instructed the instructor how to teach her by using positive reinforcement instead. Her game improved immediately and dramatically, which impressed the instructor quite a bit.

THE CRITICAL EFFECT

A baby does not learn to walk by concentrating on what it does wrong. Instead, it attempts a few steps, falls, gets up, tries something different, *and forgets about the steps that didn't work!* Encouragement and praise *for what the baby does right* is what helps the baby learn faster how to walk. Criticism at this point would greatly inhibit the process. While encouragement and praise at this stage is also popular around the world, for some reason it is quickly abandoned in favor of direct criticism as a means of behavior modification once the walking is accomplished.

Between adults, the use of criticism to improve a relationship is like using a hammer to heal a wound. It really doesn't work very well.

During my courses and lectures, I like to demonstrate the effect of criticism on the body. First, I have a volunteer hold his or her hand straight out, and I ask the person to hold it up strongly when I push down on it. Next, I tell the person to think of a self-criticism or a criticism of someone else, and then I push down on the hand again. Invariably, the person's arm becomes weaker, because his or her body has tensed up in reaction to the criticism. Conversely, when I have the person think of self-appreciation or give praise to someone else, the person's arm strengthens, because the body relaxes and the person is now able to resist the pressure of my push better. The concept is similar to that employed by martial artists who are taught to keep the body relaxed until the moment of defending or striking or moving. In a variation of this demonstration, I criticize the person silently and the person's arm weakens, and I praise silently and the arm strengthens.

In a relationship, additional effects occur when criticism is frequent and appreciation is not. Physiologically, frequent criticism causes an increase in physical tension in both parties, which decreases the ability to experience sensory pleasure. Emotionally, the first effect of increasing tension is to diminish the ability to feel pleasurable emotions, and the second effect is to increase sensitivity to more criticism. Because the subconscious mind has a natural tendency to move toward pleasure and away from pain, when criticism becomes painful, the person being criticized will suppress feelings further, causing even more tension, and move further away from the critic, either emotionally or physically or both. Meanwhile, the critic also feels less physical and emotional pleasure in the presence of the one being criticized. Unfortunately, the result is often more criticism to try to solve the problem.

I worked with a young couple whose marriage was in trouble because they were losing their positive feelings for each other and didn't know why. In our discussions, it turned out that they played a "put-down" game with each other all the time consisting of trying to outdo each other with criticisms. He would criticize her about something, then she would make a worse criticism about him, and so on. I pointed out the negative effects of criticism and the positive effects of praise, but they decided they liked their game too much to give it up. Three months later they were divorced.

While I was in the Marine Corps, two men in my unit were best friends from the same home town. They began a game called "Playing the Dozens" similar to what the couple above was doing. I will never forget coming into the barracks one day to find them trying to kill each other after a "game" session in which one of them finally couldn't take it any more.

On the other hand, I have worked with many cases where couples or friends have healed failing relationships merely by dropping or reducing criticism and increasing praise and appreciation for each other.

COPING WITH CRITICS

The word *criticism* comes directly from the Greek word *critikos*, which actually means "to discern," to be able to choose or see differences. But that is related to a Latin word, *discernere*, which means "to separate," and also to the English word *crisis*. Indeed, when you criticize you cause a crisis, and a crisis is a turning point that at a fundamental level involves separation. This is what criticism creates.

If criticism were just a matter of separating things into parts in order to look at them, it wouldn't be so bad. But criticism has become a tool for emotional manipulation by creating separation between the critics and the people being criticized. The separation causes unhappiness, pain, and fear, and people do the best they can to cope with it.

Different people cope in different ways. Some become aggressive, some become passive, some become passive-aggressive, some repress their feelings, and some of them learn to cut off all emotion and become walking zombies in order not to be hurt. Some distance themselves from others in various ways, from autism to superiority.

I know that last tactic well, because I used it for a while. When I was a kid in high school, I went through a stage of being "Mister Superior." Aloof. I thought I was projecting an image of cool, casual aloofness. However, at a party I turned around to see three girls "salaaming" me behind my back, arms out and heads down as if mocking my god-like attitude. That started some self-reflection: "Hey, wait a second, this is not quite the image I thought I was projecting." My superior stance was one reaction I had developed to protect myself from feeling criticized that didn't work very well.

Many people develop other ways of protecting their feelings. Some become pleasers, thinking that the way to be safe is to please everyone. They developed the technique originally to cope with critical parents, and they're still practicing it now out of habit. They have a fear that someone is going to get angry with them, that someone won't like them. And behind that idea is the fear that if someone doesn't like you, you're out, out of society, cast away, abandoned to starve. . . .

For fear of criticism, sometimes people will not ask for favors. Some people will not ask for an extra cup of coffee in a restaurant because the waitress might get mad; she would give them a dirty look, and they are scared to death of dirty looks, because dirty looks switch on the child's feeling of terror. They know consciously that a dirty look isn't going to hurt them, but they remember the emotional hurt of rejection, and they don't know what to do about it. So they avoid situations in which someone might rebuke them, get mad at them, or show dislike for them, because those are all forms of criticism.

To further protect themselves, some people might not accept favors freely given. My mother, who was highly sensitive to criticism of any kind, direct or implied, was like that. She was a very generous woman, but she had a terrible time receiving gifts or favors. I helped her make a breakthrough when I asked her if doing things for other people gave her pleasure. When she said it did, I asked if she loved her children. When she said that of course she did, I asked her why she was denying her children the pleasure of doing things for her. After that, it was easier to do her favors.

Some people imagine criticism when none is intended because they've been trained as a child to expect it, no matter what they do. They are so bound up with the idea that something is wrong with them that they will readily hear a critical message in whatever someone says. For instance, once when talking with a dancer I said, "You're a dancer! That's very interesting. I saw a dance group last night, and there was this one person who was really outstanding, really enjoying it. . . ." Here I was, sharing this experience because I thought she would be interested, and later

I discovered that she had been saying to herself, "He thinks that other woman is a better dancer than I am. There's something wrong with me. He's really putting me down, and I resent that."

Sometimes you can't even talk to such people about anyone else because they'll think it's a put-down. What a sad way to live! Such a person feels awful because they always compare themselves negatively with the person being discussed, no matter what the discussion is about.

Fear of criticism can be so pervasive that it's scary, especially if you start looking at all the things you do in your life based on what other people might say or do. A friend of mine once said she estimated that 90 percent of her waking life was devoted to worrying about what other people might think of her behavior. As an adult, I thought I had rid myself of that kind of fear I had learned as a child. Well, I was attending a conference with my wife not long ago, and during a break in the three-hour lecture someone led us through an aerobic exercise that we could do right there standing by our chairs. It was a great way to get the limbs moving and limber the muscles. So we're standing there, and the instructor says, "Raise your arms and wiggle your bottom." Instantly I was filled with embarrassment. It's as if a little voice inside was saying, "You're not going to move like that! What would people think? What would people say if they see you moving like that? You'll look foolish, you'll look silly." Amazed to hear this voice inside me, I replied, "Hey! Self! Everybody here is doing it! Look around! Nobody's sitting down. Everybody's waving their hands and twitching their bottom. Who's going to say anything?"

Later, I realized that my reaction had been a habit response. It had nothing to do with somebody actually standing there saying, "You're foolish." It had to do with a habit of not wanting to look foolish in general. And since I don't usually run around waving my arms and wiggling my bottom, the habitual response came up of "Ooh, ah, terrible, don't! They'll throw you out, abandon you, you'll starve to death! . . ." And so the whole sequence learned in childhood goes on. Once I was able to see that and let myself know that it was okay to act in a weird way, I had no problem. I joined in and wiggled with the best of them. But I had to deal with my old fear first. I had to let myself know consciously that there was no danger.

Developing Awareness of Criticism

Often we don't even notice how critical we and the others around us are. One excellent practice is to become more conscious of criticism, whether it originates with you or with someone else.

1. For a full week, go on a diet from criticism. Do your best not to criticize anyone or anything, aloud or mentally. That includes exempting yourself, too.

2. When someone does something wrong, if you have to say something, tell them what to do right, but don't criticize. If something goes wrong, fix it if you can, but don't criticize.

3. Pay attention to how much others around you criticize people or things or situations, but don't criticize them for it.

4. Notice how you feel when you try not to criticize. Pleased? Anxious? Helpless? Angry? Your reactions may help you discover the motives behind your criticisms.

5. If you can go a full seven days without criticizing the first time you try it, you are exceptional!

Coping with Embarrassment

Here's a way to turn what I said above about the subject of embarrassment into a technique.

1. Think of a situation in which you either felt embarrassed or imagine that you might feel embarrassed.

2. Give yourself permission to act the way you did or the way you might act, regardless of what people think.

3. Tell yourself that you won't be abandoned, you won't be cast out, and you won't starve to death because of it.

4. Repeat these steps until you can remember or imagine the incident without feeling embarrassed.

Every time you act out of fear, you reinforce the fear. Every time you do something to avoid criticism, you increase the fear of criticism until it runs your life. And if that's what is running your life, you are not a free person. You are no longer doing things out of choice. You are doing them because the "Masters" all around are telling you what to do. It's time to get your freedom back! Unless you do something illegal, no one has the right to judge you—not your parents, not anyone else—although many people will try because, subconsciously or not, they are trying to be your parent.

Coping with Substitute Parents

Substitute parents are the people who tell you how to speak, how to stand, how to sit, how to act, how to dress, and how to feel without being paid for it. They may be disguised as relatives, friends, or teachers, but they are acting like critical parents. This next technique is based on logical reinterpretation, and it works because your subconscious is very logical, once you give it an acceptable assumption.

1. Recall a time when you were criticized by a parent. There may be many such incidents; if so, apply what follows to each of them, one at a time.

2. For each incident, tell yourself strongly, "That wasn't criticism; that was an opinion. It did not mean that anything is wrong with me or that I was bad. An opinion was being expressed about my behavior, and that's all. So what?" Repeat this self-talk until you feel differently about the incident.

3. Apply this technique to any "substitute parents" in your life. The effect will be to take away the power of

the criticisms directed at you. And when they are no longer powerful they are no longer dangerous, and you no longer have the same reactions.

Coping with Critical Memories

This exercise deals directly with your feelings about a memory of being criticized. It works well for most people most of the time, but not so well for severely traumatic incidents.

1. Recall a time when you were criticized.

2. Imagine antlers growing out of the head of the person criticizing you.

3. Imagine that person dressed in a clown costume while a circus band plays music.

4. Add anything else you want to make the situation as silly and ridiculous as possible, and notice how your feelings about the incident have changed.

Here's another imaginative exercise for coping with critical memories that you might find works well:

1. Recall a time when you were being criticized.

2. Freeze the memory into a sheet of ice, or turn it into a sheet of glass.

3. Imagine a hammer in your hand, and break up the ice or glass into little pieces.

4. If it is ice, let it melt and evaporate away. If it is glass, put it in a trash can and have someone take it to the dump. Notice how your feelings have changed.

These exercises are all good strategies for how you can effectively cope with critics, whether they come from the outside or the inside.

HOW TO CRITICIZE

What do you do if someone does something wrong, and the only way you know how to correct the situation is to criticize the person? If you absolutely must criticize, then you may as well do it in the most effective way possible.

The Open-Face Sandwich Technique

This technique works well because people are more open to receiving criticism when their accomplishments are acknowledged.

1. Make the necessary criticism without anger and with a clear indication of how you want it to be corrected.
2. Compliment the person on something else, no matter how small or even apparently insignificant, that he or she accomplished in a good manner.

The concept behind this technique is simple. As I described above, criticism causes tension, and praise relaxes. A person who receives praise for an accomplishment is much more likely to be receptive to a criticism and make corrections. The key, though, is to criticize first and praise second. I know this goes against the typical pattern of praising first—if you praise at all—and ending with the criticism, but physiologically and psychologically the pattern I describe is more effective.

One of my best examples of this technique occurred when my wife was the consultant for the dietary departments of a large chain of hospitals. Part of her job was to make reports to the State of California on the condition of the kitchens. On her first visit to a hospital that her corporation had just acquired, she found the kitchen in deplorable condition and employee morale very low. It was common for a person in my wife's position to fill the report with everything that was wrong, without paying attention to what might be right. In fact, noting anything good was uncommon. My wife, however, knew the effects of praise, so she searched the kitchen high and low for anything that had been done right. She finally found a faucet that was clean and bright and noted this one good thing prominently in her report. The kitchen staff was pleasantly shocked to find that anything good had been acknowledged, and that was the beginning of a turnaround for the kitchen operation and for employee morale.

The Closed-Face Sandwich Technique

This technique is similar to the above and even more effective. It does, though, take a little more effort and creativity.

1. Give a compliment.

2. Give a criticism.

3. Give a compliment.

People who encounter the two "sandwich" techniques for the first time are often afraid that giving compliments along with criticism will diminish the force or the importance of the criticism, when in fact the opposite is true. If the critic consciously or unconsciously uses criticism as a control technique, he or she may find it harder to apply the sandwiches.

THE POWER OF PRAISE

The words *praise* and *compliment* are so similar in English that they are used interchangeably, although *praise* has a stronger and more personal connotation. You can compliment a woman on her hairdo or a man on his watch, but you wouldn't usually say you were praising them. Nevertheless, I will use whichever word I feel is suitable for the sentence.

Praise is powerful because it makes you feel good. More accurately, I ought to say that it makes your body feel good. Your mind is another matter. Your body will always feel good when you receive praise, *unless* your personal or cultural rules discourage verbal praise as bad or socially unacceptable. In that case, you may feel embarrassed or worse when someone openly compliments you. On the other hand, silent or telepathic compliments that bypass your conscious mind will always make your body feel good. The same holds true when you praise other people. When someone you know has difficulty accepting praise or compliments, just do it silently. Their body will accept it happily, and their mind won't interfere.

A Silent Praise Experience

Try this simple experiment on yourself to feel the effect.

1. Mentally compliment your entire body from the top of your head all the way to the bottom of your feet, including skin, bones, organs, and everything else you can think of. An easy way to do this is to say something like, "Thank you skin for covering my body, thank you brain for thinking, thank you heart for pumping my blood," etc.

2. When you've finished with your body, compliment your less tangible attributes such as skills and talents, imagination and memory.

3. Notice how your body reacts and whether you feel calm or excited.

The power of praise stems from the connection it makes you feel to those giving the praise, even when it is you praising yourself; it is this sense of connection that feels so good and releases tension, which in turn feels good, too. The sense of connection may be variously interpreted as being loved, admired, appreciated, acknowledged, recognized, and so on. Since people tend to move toward pleasure and away from pain, praise is a good motivator, except when it is insincere. In most cases, your body can feel when praise is insincere, and then it does not have the same response. Some people, however—including some actors, performers, and dictators—are so desperate for any kind of connection that they will accept all sorts of insincere or even forced praise.

As powerful as praise is, and as good as it feels, a surprising number of people don't know how to do it. Here is an excerpt from a booklet on blessing I wrote called, "The Little Pink Booklet of Aloha." In this booklet and elsewhere, I equate blessing with compliments and praise:

> Blessing may be done with imagery or touch, but the most usual and easy way to do it is with words. The main kinds of verbal blessing are:
>
> **Admiration**. This is the giving of compliments or praise to something good that you notice, e.g., "What a beautiful sunset"; "I like that flower"; "You are such a wonderful person."
>
> **Affirmation**. This is a specific statement of blessing for increase or endurance, e.g., "I bless the beauty of this tree"; "Blessed be the health of your body."
>
> **Appreciation**. This is an expression of gratitude that something good exists or has happened, e.g., "Thank you for helping me"; I give thanks to the rain for nourishing the land."

Anticipation. This is blessing for the future, e.g., "We're going to have a great picnic"; "I bless your increased income"; "Thank you for my perfect mate"; "I wish you a happy journey"; "May the wind be always at your back."

In order to gain the most benefit from blessing, you must give up or cut way down on the one thing that negates it: cursing. This doesn't mean swearing or saying "bad" words. It refers to the opposite of blessing: namely, criticizing instead of admiring; doubting instead of affirming; blaming instead of appreciating; and worrying instead of anticipating with trust. Any of these actions tend to cancel out the effects of blessing. The more you curse, the harder gaining the good from a blessing will be and the longer it will take. On the other hand, the more you bless, the less harm cursing will do. Here, then, are some ideas for blessing various needs and desires. Apply them as often as you like, as much as you want:

Health. Bless healthy people, animals, and even plants; everything that is well made or well constructed; and everything that expresses abundant energy.

Happiness. Bless all that is good or the good in all people and all things; all the signs of happiness that you see, hear, or feel in people or animals; and all potentials for happiness that you notice around you.

Prosperity. Bless all the signs of prosperity in your environment, including everything that money helped to make or do; all the money that you have in any form; and all the money that circulates in the world.

Success. Bless all signs of achievement and completion (such as buildings, bridges, and sports events); all arrivals at destinations (of ships, planes, trains, cars, and people); all signs of forward movement or persistence; and all signs of enjoyment or fun.

Confidence. Bless all signs of confidence in people and animals; all signs of strength in people, animals and objects (including steel and concrete); all signs of stability (like mountains and tall trees); and all signs of purposeful power (including big machines, power lines, and so on).

Love and Friendship. Bless all signs of caring and nurturing, compassion and support; all harmonious relationships in nature and architecture; everything that is connected to or gently touching something else; all signs of cooperation, as in games or work; and all signs of laughter and fun.

Inner Peace. Bless all signs of quietness, calmness, tranquility, and serenity (such as quiet water or still air); all distant views (horizons, stars, the moon); all signs of beauty of sight, sound, or touch; clear colors and shapes; the details of natural or made objects.

Spiritual Growth. Bless all signs of growth, development, and change in nature; the transitions of dawn and twilight; the movement of sun, moon, planets, and stars; the flight of birds; and the movement of wind and sea.

The previous ideas are for guidance if you are not used to blessing, but don't be limited by them. Remember that any quality, characteristic, or condition can be blessed (e.g., you can bless slender poles and slim animals to encourage weight loss), whether it has existed, presently exists, or exists so far in your imagination alone.

Personally, I have used the power of blessing to heal my body, increase my income, develop many skills, create a deeply loving relationship with my wife and children, and establish a worldwide network of peacemakers working with the aloha spirit. It is because this blessing power has worked so well for me that I want to share it with you. Please share it with as many others as you can.

Chapter 3

The Art of Forgiveness

Forgiveness is one of the most beautiful experiences you can have. If you don't think so now, I hope you will by the end of this chapter. Forgiveness is not only beautiful in itself for the feeling that arises when you forgive someone or something, it is also beautiful because of the greater results it brings about.

The word for "forgiveness" in Hawaiian is *kala*, and it contains several interesting meanings. One of the most important is the meaning of release, which is the essence of forgiveness. A common misconception is that forgiveness is done for the wrongdoer. While that person may indeed benefit, especially if he or she is in danger of punishment otherwise, the main beneficiary will be the person doing the forgiving, because true forgiving releases all the anger and tension that may be held around the issue. Anger contains a great deal of energy that you may inwardly block in the effort to keep holding it against someone—including yourself. The act of forgiving can dispel this anger, releasing tremendous energy for you to put into the direction or path you want to go. The result can be the full awakening of your inner powers and increased happiness beyond anything you ever dreamed possible.

Some people would think that statement outrageous. But consider that anger, guilt, and resentment all cause excessive tension; and that excessive physical tension interferes with the functioning of body, mind, and spirit, thus inhibiting your access to happiness and your inner powers.

THE PROCESS OF TRUE FORGIVENESS

What is true forgiveness? First, I will tell you what true forgiveness is not: It is not simply saying the words, "I forgive you." That is only a formal way of acknowledging forgiveness; it is not the act of forgiveness itself. Forgiveness can occur without any words at all.

Technically speaking, forgiveness is the act of deciding not to punish, or to wish punishment, for what someone did. Realistically, on the other hand, forgiveness is the state in which you no longer feel angry about the wrongdoing. It is also the process by which you reach that state. There are many ways to forgive and many techniques that can be applied, but forgiveness only happens when a particular process occurs. Here's how it goes:

1. Someone does something that breaks one of your serious rules.

2. You get angry (in the form of simple anger, rage, jealousy, envy, resentment, or feelings of betrayal, guilt, etc.).

3. You want the person to be punished in some way (physically, emotionally, mentally).

4. Then, for some reason or another, you change your mind about how you feel about the person and/or the event.

As most of us probably know, this last step is often not easily reached, and why forgiving is so difficult is very important to understand. The difficulty in forgiving someone is usually based on the ideas you have about forgiveness. Here are some common ideas that make forgiveness difficult:

1. You believe that what the person did was unforgivable, and you refuse to change your mind about that.

2. You believe that by forgiving, you would be doing the person a favor, and you really don't want to do that.

3. You believe that forgiving means forgetting, and you are afraid that if you forgot the incident you would allow the same or similar things to happen to you again.

Let's look at these three ideas in turn.

Forgiving the Unforgivable

You have the right to keep any rules about right and wrong, good and bad, that you have. Likewise, you have the right never to forgive someone, including yourself, for something done or not done. The problem is not with being unforgiving. The problem is with the consequences thereof, for as long as you remain unforgiving your inner tension will increase, year by year, with increasingly serious physical, emotional, and mental effects. It would seem at first glance that you are in a double-bind: either to pay the price of not forgiving or to pay the same price—ever-increasing tension—by betraying your deepest values.

Here, I'm mainly talking about the tension-filled energy that builds up from hatred. The word *hate* scares some people, but a euphemism like "intense dislike" just doesn't carry the same feeling. It is ongoing hatred that makes something seem unforgivable. Some people who are pretty tough can handle chronic hatred for quite a few years before the body begins to break down. More sensitive people experience the negative effects of hate-tension almost immediately. Many factors are involved, but forgiveness is the one factor that can release such tension.

It doesn't matter how old you are. I know people in their seventies who still hate their parents, and that hatred interferes with their happiness, even at that age. Somehow or other, they have to release the stranglehold that the parental image still has on them. The parents might be gone physically, but as long as they still exist in the mind, along with the hatred for what they did or didn't do, they continue to control a person's life.

Regarding parents, here are some ideas that might be helpful: Realize, first of all, that your parents are not God. They weren't ever intended to be. They are just normal human beings with their own fears, misunderstandings, and ideas for how to do things. However they may have botched things up, they were doing the best they could, based on who they were and what they believed. If you can acknowledge this, you will be taking a step forward, because now you may be able to forgive them for being so ignorant of good parenting. Or forgive them for not knowing how to love you better. Or maybe you can simply forgive them for being stupid. Forgiving them means, "I release you from any desire for punishment, for having been so stupid." You don't have to release them for having hurt you. But if you can release them for anything specific, then you can begin to realize that everything else was just a consequence of their stupidity or ignorance, or for not knowing how to act differently, or for just being mean by nature, or for whatever else may have been at the root of their wrongdoing.

To the extent that you can forgive such people—whether they be parents, friends, employers, spouses, or others—for some aspect of their behavior or beliefs (like not knowing how to relate better, trying too hard, not being strong, or things over which they may not have had any control), that forgiveness will release the pressure on you. It will also release the tension between you and them or your memories of them. And then more of your energy will be released for your own health and happiness.

Of course, it is easy to tell someone to forgive, while carrying that forgiveness out is not always easy. So I'm not merely telling you to forgive someone you hate; I am going to tell you how.

Forgiving the Forgivable

My solution to the problem of resisting forgiveness is unusual, admittedly, but it does work. I know, because I have used it. In my life I have encountered people who did terrible things, either to me or to those I love. Yet, by forgiving in a particular way, I became free of tension around the issue, even though I still realized that what the person did was terrible. In case my technique can work for others, here it is:

1. Acknowledge that what the person did was wrong, very wrong, that it always was and always will be wrong.

2. At the same time, forgive the person for some aspect of their behavior, character, or knowledge that you can find forgivable, whether it is directly related to the main incident or not.

3. Repeat this exercise, changing the wording as necessary, until you can think of this aspect of the person without feeling any anger or tension.

The key to making this process work is to focus only on forgiving what you *can* forgive. Instead of trying to forgive a terrible deed, you forgive something about the person that is less important. To the degree that you can change your thinking about any aspect of the person or the incident in a way that relieves your feeling about it, you will be free of that much tension.

Forgiving as a Favor

The more powerless a person feels, the more likely he or she is to think that forgiving someone is the same as giving them the power to act the same way again. This is not the case at all.

Forgiving is an internal act that affects you more than anyone else. And the greatest effect it has on you is to increase or return your own power to you. It confers no benefit whatsoever to the other person unless, as mentioned above, they care how you feel or it helps them avoid punishment.

Moreover, forgiving a person does not necessarily exempt them from deserved punishment. Let's say, for instance, that someone did something to you that involves a lawsuit. You can forgive that person and still pursue the lawsuit, because you are pursuing your rights under the law. What matters, in terms of your emotional and mental health, is the spirit in which you do it. If you pursue the lawsuit in a spirit of revenge, the whole thing will backfire on you. But if you go at it with a common-sense acknowledgment of asserting whatever just rights you have, you will be much more successful.

So again, the point is not *what* you do but the spirit in which you do it. Yes, there is a fine line between seeking justice and seeking revenge, but it's a vital line in terms of your happiness and your effectiveness. If you really want to be effective in a legal dispute, you must be clear about your goal. If it is to redress a grievance, to make things as right as they can be, and to obtain some justice, the pursuit is worthy and honorable. Most legal systems are set up for that. On the other hand, if you are out to punish the other person or to make them cry for mercy, as much as you might feel justified in that goal, it won't be effective for you in the long term. This is true whether the situation is legal or strictly personal. When you feel resentment toward your parents, a lover, a friend, or even the world in general, typically you constantly dwell on it. That feeling of resentment in turn makes you angry. And the more you dwell on that anger, the more blocked energy you build up and the less effective you become.

My point here, of course, is that it doesn't have to be this way, even though revenge does have a very seductive quality that can make it hard to resist. In the United States, popular ideas are often stated on bumper stickers. One that was popular for a while was, "Don't get mad, get even." I never understood why people would be so drawn to that idea until one of my sons was talking about getting revenge on one of his friends and I said, "Now tell me, would that really make you feel good?"

"Yeah!" he replied.

When I thought about that and talked with him some more, I realized he was right: exacting revenge truly would result in a good feeling—temporarily. No doubt about it. And the temporary good feeling would come from the sense of somehow being effective in that moment. You have felt helpless, you have felt out of control, and getting even is a way of feeling in control again.

But that sense of power is false, because its only effectiveness is in giving you that temporary jolt of good feeling, like a drug would. In terms of changing situations, it's not effective, because the problem will just return, either with that person or someone else. When the energy of revenge is sent out, it has to come back, usually in the form of a backlash of more revenge, a lifelong vendetta, or a feud that lasts for centuries. It is not an effective technique for changing your feelings. There are better ways to be assertive, to do what you feel is clearly right, and yet not use the energy of destruction to do it.

Some people actually believe that by not forgiving they are punishing the other person. They may believe that withholding forgiveness gives them a sort of power over the other. In this case their motive is manipulative. Although the person withholding forgiveness must still deal with the tension, the person not being forgiven may react with fear or emotional hurt, if they care about how the manipulator feels. However, you readers who are victims of such manipulation need not be affected much longer, because later I will tell you how to get free of this trap.

In forgiving people, remember that you are not saying that what they did was right or good. Instead, you are releasing them because your feelings of anger or resentment have been holding you back. You are releasing the energy that's keeping you sometimes poor, sometimes unsuccessful, sometimes unhealthy, sometimes without a good relationship—and that's all you're doing. What you do now, today, and intend to do tomorrow is much more important than anything that happened in the past.

The powerful idea I want to share now is for you to give permission for someone else to be the way they are and do what they do. Or to be the way they were and do what they did. That act of giving permission in itself is an act of forgiveness. And the effect that can suddenly result is miraculous. It can also release all the problems of disappointment, because how can you be disappointed with someone if you've already given them permission to be who they are and to do what they do? While their behavior may give you a few moments of disillusionment or even disappointment, the feeling doesn't last long if you remember, "Wait a second! I gave them permission to be what they are and do what they do. So whatever they do, even though I don't like it, I don't have to stay disappointed."

Just as forgiveness in the form of giving permission frees you from disappointment, it also frees you from resentment, since resentment is based in disappointment. Think about what disappointment really means. It is no more than the feeling that comes when things don't turn out the way you wanted. You thought something was going to be a certain way, and it wasn't, and so you feel angry or resentful. Feeling that way for a few moments is understandable, but why let it limit you from moving forward in the future? Is it because you are afraid of being disappointed again? I've met an amazing number of people who avoid potentially happy relationships because they might be disappointed. That doesn't make a lot of sense, given that in order to feel disappointed you must choose to feel bad when something happens that you don't like.

Giving Permission

Here is a technique that will help you to forgive without fear and to feel more powerful at the same time.

Oddly enough, while practicing it may seem as if you are doing the other person a favor, it is really you yourself who is the beneficiary.

1. Think of a situation in which you have decided to forgive a person but are afraid to do so or don't know how.

2. Imagine that you are the Rule Maker of the Universe. Out of the generosity of your heart, give the person permission to be and do what he or she is and does, or to have been and done the same.

3. From now on, whenever you think of what happened, remind yourself that you have given permission. The effect, over time, is to diminish any fear you may have around the situation and to transfer its power to you, as far as feeling goes.

Forgiving and Forgetting

The idea behind the admonition to "forgive and forget" is misunderstood. Forgiving is not the same as forgetting. The real basis for the adage is the fact that, when you truly forgive something, it may become so unimportant that you forget about it.

Unfortunately, when forgiveness is needed, many people try to forget by refusing to think about the incident. While it may be good not to dwell on something that needs forgiving, the problem is that suppressing it does not truly prevent dwelling on it. The sense of injury is constantly there in the subconscious awareness. It keeps trying to surface so that the person can resolve it; but he or she keeps pretending it's not there, even though they know it is, with the result that no forgiveness takes place. And forgetting is not happening, either.

Sometimes forgetting about an offense completely, even if you do forgive, can work in your worst interests. If you forgive someone for some harm and then forget about it so completely that you can't remember it, you may find yourself in the same situation again. If a person has swindled you out of half your life's savings and you decide to forgive and forget, the same person has a good chance of swindling you out of the other half. I have a number of friends who have done moderate harm to me and to my organization. We are still friends now for two reasons: because I have forgiven them and because I remember what happened. I give my friends permission to make mistakes so that we can still be friends. But I do my best to make sure that the same mistakes won't be made again, at least around me. That way I can continue to enjoy those aspects of our friendship that still work.

On the other hand, pretending to forget can actually lead to healing in some cases. During my work in Senegal, West Africa, I established a reputation in the diplomatic and business communities for my negotiating skills. It happened that an American company had made a contract with the Senegalese government to drill for wells in a particular province. However, no one had notified the quasi-autonomous military governor of that province, so he promptly jailed all the Americans on site and confiscated their equipment. Negotiations between the governor, the American Embassy, and the central government of Senegal made no headway, because the governor would not forgive the slight to his authority.

That's when I was asked to help. First, I made an appointment to see the governor, without specifying the purpose. Next I met with the president of the American company and told him to let me do the talking and to trust me no matter what I said. Then the president and I went to see the governor.

To the American president the whole event seemed surreal. I greeted the governor, whom I already knew, and introduced the president. I told the governor that the president's company was interested in helping the governor find more water for the agricultural activities of his province. The governor said he thought that sounded like a good idea. Finally, the governor and I set a date for the beginning of the project.

At no time was the existing situation mentioned, although the governor and I both knew what it was, and we both knew that we knew. Even as we were talking, the American workers were in jail and the American equipment was sitting in a provincial warehouse. The governor and I, however, both pretended nothing had happened, which allowed us to negotiate without any history to deal with.

After the meeting, the company president was furious with me for not dealing with what he thought was the problem, which was that of his men and his equipment. I told him that the real problem was the affront to the governor's authority. Now that we had dealt with that, the other problems would be resolved. His trust in me was shaky at first, but two weeks later he accompanied me to the drilling site, and there were his men and his equipment, all set up and ready to go!

By maintaining an awareness of the unpleasant event without bringing it up, the governor and I were able to start over without rancor or criticism or blame. The effect was to desensitize the event, and taking away its emotional charge gave us the freedom to move forward. The same approach may work for you in your relations with friends, as long as those friends value the friendship more than their need to be right.

As mentioned above, the more unimportant an event becomes, the easier it is to forget it in a natural way. In a technique for forgiveness, then, the emphasis is on disempowering the event, rather than on forgetting it.

TIME-SHIFT FORGIVENESS

This technique works well as a means of forgiving—that is, changing your mind and feelings about—a person or an event that is no longer part of your current life.

1. Think about the event you want to forgive. Then be aware of your current situation.

2. Remind yourself that what happened then is no longer important because it no longer exists.

3. Repeat this process every time the event comes to mind.

PARTIAL FORGIVENESS

Sometimes a relationship problem seems so big that the idea of forgiving is too overwhelming. In that case, you can begin by forgiving a little bit and work your way up to more. There's no cosmic law that says you have to forgive everything all at once. You can do it in bits and pieces, a little at a time, as long as you get started.

One of my clients had a very difficult time forgiving her husband for something. The tremendous tension she experienced was producing severe physical problems, but she still didn't feel she could forgive him. So she and I came up with the idea that she could at least send a ball of love or forgiveness—a little pink ball about an inch in diameter—for one second. She could do that much. I'd have negotiated down to a nanosecond if necessary, and had the ball be a millimeter in diameter, just to get her to do something, because she had been doing absolutely nothing before.

After weeks of continually sending that one-inch ball of pink light to her husband, she gradually became able to send a six-foot ball of light for one whole minute! As a result, her body began to loosen up; she was feeling freer of the aches and pains and insecurities that she'd been causing herself by her attitude. Here is the exercise for you to try yourself:

1. Think of a person you want to forgive but can't seem to do so completely.

2. Make a decision to forgive that person just a tiny bit for a small amount of time, such as one second.

3. Imagine a symbol for that forgiveness. It could be a one-inch or one-centimeter ball of pink light, a single note of music, or anything else that appeals to you.

4. Imagine sending or giving this small bit of forgiveness to the person in question.

5. Continue to do this exercise on a regular basis, gradually increasing the time or the size or the notes or whatever as you are able, until the forgiveness feels complete.

SELF-FORGIVENESS

Self-forgiveness is needed when you have a problem with guilt. Guilt occurs when you believe you have done something wrong or when you feel that something about you is wrong. The latter leads to feelings of inadequacy and then to feelings of guilt, because you don't know what to do about it.

If it's a question of having actually *done* something wrong, then you can either correct the wrong, if possible, or use some of the techniques above to forgive yourself. But if it's a question of feeling guilty because you believe you are inadequate in your very being, a different approach is required.

Often, parents create a sense of inadequacy by making the child responsible for their happiness. Other family members, authority figures, and even friends, lovers, or spouses may do the same thing. The notion puts the person into an impossible position, because he or she has no control over another person's feelings. When this happens, the basic message is, "You are responsible for my happiness. If I'm not happy, there's something wrong with you and you can't have my love."

In undertaking the impossible task of pleasing parents or anyone else in order to survive and to be loved, many people grow up feeling really defective, as if something is truly wrong with them. Because that's such a devastating idea, they may react by directing anger toward the one needing to be pleased, but under the anger is the sense of personal inadequacy. Transforming that sense into one instead of personal *adequacy*—of being loved and loveable—can give people a sense of power to fulfill their dreams, to be and do what they want to be and do. But where is that sense of adequacy to come from?

Many people search the world for someone to support and love them while not doing the same thing for themselves. Well, folks, if you are one of these people I hate to disappoint you, but it just isn't going to happen. Life doesn't work that way. You will find some real masters of living in the world who can love you in spite of you, but for the most part you will find people who simply react to you the way you react to yourself. If you have a sense of something being wrong with you, you broadcast it subtly both through your behavior and telepathically, and others will relate to you accordingly. Feeling loved and supported in the world begins with self-loving. By learning how to love yourself, you assume responsibility for your own happiness, regardless of what others might say or do.

You can begin with as simple a thing as telling yourself "I love you," no matter how you actually feel about yourself right now. You can talk to your body first, telling various parts of it—your head, your hands, your feet, your skin, your bones, your hair, your organs, and all the rest—"I like you, I love you, you're pretty nice." Even if at first you don't quite mean it, and even if it feels a little silly, so what? The rewards of silliness are sometimes well worth it.

Then you might talk to your mind and tell it the same thing. You might talk to your soul and your spirit and your energy and whatever else, somehow telling yourself as a whole, "Hey, I like you! I think you're pretty nice. I think you're okay, no matter what happened. No matter what you've done, I love you."

I can already hear objections, the loudest one being, "How can I love myself if I know I don't deserve it?" The short answer is, "Just do it anyway." The long answer is, "You have to practice unconditional love." That is such an important aspect of forgiveness, and especially of self-forgiveness, that I must discuss it more in depth.

UNCONDITIONAL LOVE

If we were to search for the "highest," most consistent, cross-cultural, ethical, philosophical, and spiritual guideline for living, it would probably be "to love one another." Not only is this idea found all over the earth, but, according to many sources, even aliens are telling us to do it.

It's an easy thing to say, and it feels like the right thing to do, but how do we really love one another in a world of lies, deceit, murder, abuse, torture, ignorance, and people who are simply irritating? How do we get from the words to the act without just acting a part and being false to our real feelings?

Actually, we could start by acting a part with good effect. Pretending to love each other is a lot better than killing each other, after all. We can see this approach in practice at diplomatic functions, whenever a losing team cheers the winning one, and when beauty contest runner-ups congratulate the new queen. If we are observant, we can see it in personal relationships as well. However, the problem with this solution is that it is extremely stressful, both for the pretender and the pretendee, and especially in long-term relationships. Our subconscious is very aware of the true feelings within and around us, even when our conscious mind denies them. There has to be a better way.

Another solution offered by some is called "unconditional love." The idea is to remove all judgments in your thinking and feelings of good and bad, right and wrong, pleasurable and painful, etc. Then, so the teaching goes, you will be able to love everyone and everything equally, under all conditions and in all situations.

Unfortunately, this idea is not really a solution; it's an idealization. A solution to a problem implies a method or plan for achieving a resolution. Proposing unconditional love as a solution to human relationships is like saying, "If only people would stop fighting we could all live in peace." Yeah, right, so how do we do that? How do we get from conditional to unconditional love? If the only method is years and years of meditative exercises, then this is not a viable solution, either, for the majority of individuals living their daily lives or for society as a whole.

Another difficulty with the concept of unconditional love, as nice as it sounds, is precisely that it's *unconditional*. Think about it: no conditions at all! No rules or laws for human behavior—no incentive for healing or caring, or creativity and invention; no reason for loving one person more than another, no matter how they look or act; no desire for learning or teaching or challenge—because all of these things require judgment of some kind. The end result of unconditional love would be like living in the Garden of Eden again. Some people think that would be great; some think that getting kicked out of the nest was the best thing that ever happened to Adam and Eve, as hard as it's been.

Finally, let's put unconditional love to rest with a very practical consideration. Any solution to the problem of how to love one another has to be progressive. In other words, it has to start somewhere and grow. Regardless of what you think about it, for unconditional love to work in a widespread way would require some sort of magical, instant transformation of everyone at the same time. Otherwise, all those conditional people would make life extremely difficult and dangerous for their lovers and friends and neighbors who were trying to be unconditional. On the other hand, the latter probably wouldn't even notice, if they survived. This is probably why those who practice unconditional love usually start out in caves and on mountaintops, far from where most people live.

I believe that we can learn to love each other to a far greater degree than we do. So as an alternative to the unrealistic ideal of unconditional love, I encourage creative conditional love instead. This approach is conditional because it recognizes the usefulness of having comparisons of good and bad, right and wrong, and so on. It is creative because it allows for changing those judgments when they are no longer useful. This concept allows for a way to love one another that works, that is simple, and that doesn't take a lot of effort. The trouble is that it usually isn't easy.

It's easy to love people who make us feel good. It's easy to love a smiling baby, children playing happily, or helpful adults. It can be very hard to love a screaming baby, destructive children, or arrogant adults. It might be nice to be able to step instantly into unconditional love, but it is more practical to think in terms of expanding our love from where it is now, maybe even by just a little bit at a time. Just as a long journey begins with the first step, the road to loving one another can start with one instance of more tolerance or with one unrewarded act of kindness.

The experience of learning how to love one another may be active or passive. Active loving is doing something for the benefit of someone else. It can have a personal benefit, too, but for it to be *active* loving, the intent to benefit another must be primary. Many things we do out of habit or obligation could become acts of love if we would only think of whom they benefit. Paying bills or paying taxes, for instance, could become acts of love if, when you paid them, you thought of all the food, shelter, and clothing you were providing to people dependent on your payments. Even inhaling could become an act of love if you did it with the thought of giving oxygen to your cells, and exhaling could be an act of love if you did it with the thought of feeding the plants of the world.

Passive loving starts with tolerance and slowly moves its way up to appreciation. The way to increase tolerance is to eliminate some of your rules. Almost everyone has rules about right and wrong, good and bad, possible and impossible, etcetera and etcetera. When someone breaks one of our rules, we tend to get upset and either nurse our anger, criticize the rule breaker, or commit violence against them. Sometimes we do all three. The rules that lead to this effect most often contain the words *should* or *shouldn't*. It's easy to get angry with someone who should have done something and didn't, or who should not have done something and did. I have at various times become upset with someone who was not on time for a meeting or who did not complete a task I wanted them to do.

It's bad enough when we have too many of our own "should" and "shouldn't" rules, but we become silly when we start taking on other people's rules of that kind. A few years ago I caught myself getting angry on a golf course because someone was walking on a pathway reserved for golf carts, regardless of the sign forbidding it. When I realized what I was doing, I was shocked at my own behavior. Not only was it not my golf course, the person was neither harming nor endangering anyone. That day I discovered that one of my own rules was that people should not break other people's rules. Far from being useful, it was making me unnecessarily intolerant and giving me unnecessary stress. I got rid of that rule, but I did keep the one I have about not doing things that are obviously dangerous or harmful to innocent bystanders. However, that's my rule, and it doesn't matter whether anyone else has a similar rule or not. Now I am no longer a watchdog for other people's rules.

There's a funny thing about loving one another. It gets easier to do the more you love yourself. The biblical commandment to "love thy neighbor as thyself" assumes a precondition that most people miss. Almost everyone focuses on the "love thy neighbor" part. I ask you to focus on the "as thyself" part for a moment. Whether you think of it as a commandment or just a good idea, it presupposes that loving begins with yourself and that this self-love is the reference you have for loving your neighbor (meaning anyone in your vicinity, by the way). Also, the implication is that you think well of yourself, because if you hated yourself you would hate your neighbor. I have to admire how cleverly the author of these words incorporated the necessity for self-esteem into such a short guideline for human relationships.

Hence, in regard to one relationship in particular I firmly believe that it is wise and right and good to get as close to unconditional love as we possibly can—and that relationship is with oneself. The more you love yourself unconditionally, the happier and more effective you will be in all circumstances.

Loving yourself unconditionally is more important than trying to love anyone else unconditionally. If you can't love yourself unconditionally, forget about trying to love anyone else that way. You will fall short, and then you will feel bad about yourself for falling short. If you start loving yourself unconditionally, then other people will begin to respond to you in the same way. And, in practical terms, the more you love yourself honestly and sincerely, without needing to compare yourself to anyone else, the less others will criticize you.

There is a fact of existence that you would do well to understand. In this life of yours, there will be some people—speaking of parents, friends, strangers, or anyone else—who will love you depending on what you do; there will be some people who will not love you depending on what you do; there will be some people who will love you no matter what you do; and there will be some people who will not love you no matter what you do. And some of these people may change their minds at any time.

It makes no sense, therefore, to put your whole sense of being loved or loveable, having self-esteem or self-worth, and feeling accepted or connected entirely in the hands of others. Nor does it make sense to rely on others for forgiveness of your faults and mistakes. If people do love you and like you and forgive you, that's nice. But you don't have to let your happiness depend on it.

Self-love is equal to self-forgiveness. And self-love in the sense of simply acknowledging your own goodness, reminding yourself of it, telling it to yourself frequently, is something you can do whenever you choose. You can do it in front of a mirror if you like, but you don't have to wait until you are in front of a mirror. Do it anytime. If you get angry at yourself, just say, "Oh, that's okay, I love you anyway." If you make a mistake, say, "Oh, that's okay, don't worry about it, I love you anyway." If you become angry and embarrass yourself by storming and raging and going into a funk, as soon as you can become aware say, "Oh, that doesn't matter, I love you anyway." You will be beautifully surprised at how quickly your negative feelings diminish and how easily this kind of positive self-talk can become a habit.

A SELF-FORGIVENESS EXERCISE

This exercise is actually called *ho'oponopono iki* in Hawaiian. Ho'oponopono is an ancient practice that evolved as a means of family therapy and group reconciliation, as well as a means of harmonizing any kind of relationship. In my book, *Instant Healing*, I go into great detail about this technique. The more or less standard format for it involves a group leader, but here is a simple way to do it for yourself:

1. Take a deep breath, and let your body relax as best you can.

2. As you inhale, say your own name mentally.

3. As you exhale, say, "I release you" or "I forgive you." You can be as specific as you like. If your name is Shirley, you might say something like, "Shirley, I forgive you for what you did at the party last night."

4. Do the whole process, combining breath and statements, at least three times, or until you feel better about yourself.

CHAPTER 3

We create the reality of our experience. This concept is not something esoteric; it is something very practical and down to earth, because one of the most important ways in which we create our experience is by our attitudes and reactions to people and things and places. Just as we create our own feelings of misery and pain, we can also create our own feelings of freedom and happiness. And one of the ways to do that is by forgiving ourselves and forgiving others.

Part 2

YOUR MOST
INTIMATE
RELATIONSHIPS

Chapter 4

Your Relationship with Your Body

You might find it odd that we are talking about your body in a book on relationships, but it is your body with whom you have your earliest, most intimate relationship, even before the one you have with your mother. As a human being, you live by means of your body, and you die by means of your body. And it is the state of your body that has the greatest influence on all the rest of your relationships, because it affects how you behave toward others and how they behave toward you. Since your relationship with your body is such an important one, I'm going to start by helping you to get to know it better.

BODY AWARENESS

Breathing is probably the most important function of your body. I say this because it is the one function you can least do without. At the same time, it is the one most people know the least about.

The primary purpose of breathing seems simple enough: to provide your body with enough oxygen to keep your cells alive and well and to provide a means for expelling gaseous toxins. You can read the details about that in any good book on physiology, however. I'm more interested in having you become more aware of your breathing.

Do you know how often you breathe when you are not thinking about it? Do you know how deeply you breathe when you are not paying attention to it? Do you notice that you start to breathe more deeply and more frequently when you read or hear someone speak about breathing? Have you ever realized that your breathing becomes shallower when you are under stress, especially when you are afraid or angry? Do you know that different parts of your body tighten up or relax, depending on how you breathe? Did you know that other people notice, consciously or subconsciously, the effects of your breathing on your body and that they react by changing their behavior?

The "normal" breathing rate for adults at rest is about twelve breaths per minute. Perhaps because of my training in various breathing techniques, mine are about half that. However, "normal" rates of anything are usually taken from "average" rates, and average numbers of anything are just all the separate numbers for the matter in question added together and divided by two. So what's really normal for one person may be quite different for someone else.

More important than the rate, though, is the depth of breathing—in other words, breathing in a way that causes more oxygen to enter your system. If your breathing is very shallow, then a lot of your breathing effort is wasted, because the air never gets to the part of your body where the oxygen can be absorbed. You can have a nice, normal breathing rate of twelve breaths per minute, and all the while your body is not getting enough oxygen and the toxins are building up. Aside from these strictly physical effects, regular inadequate breathing will make you more prone to anxiety and irritation, both of which will have definite effects on your relationships, including the one with yourself.

A Conscious Breathing Exercise

There are many, many breathing techniques taught around the world for physical health, skill training, mental creativity, spiritual development, and whatever other reason human beings can think up. I'm not going to give you a special breathing technique right now (maybe later). The purpose of this exercise is simply to increase your awareness of your own breathing and its effects.

1. Breathe any way you like and be aware of what you are doing. You don't have to use any particular pattern or counting system. In all likelihood, though, you will spontaneously begin to breathe more deeply and even sigh more often. Keep this up for at least one minute.

2. In addition to the breathing itself, pay attention to anything that happens or changes in your body. Notice feelings and sensations, degrees of tension or relaxation, energy level, changes in your thoughts, etc. Shift your

attention to different parts of your body, from head to toes, in order to increase your awareness.

3. Practice changing your breathing pattern in any way you choose, and notice how that affects your body.

4. Practice changing your breathing pattern when you are with other people, and notice whether they change their behavior in any way.

Generally speaking, breathing more slowly and more deeply more often will help you to feel calmer and more confident.

MOVEMENT AWARENESS

How you move your body also affects how you feel and how other people behave toward you. In this case, movement includes "static movement," or posture.

First, let's consider movement itself. One way to become aware of your own movement patterns is to observe how other people move. This will automatically help you pay more attention to how you yourself move. Watch how other people sit down and get up, how they reach for things and pick them up or handle them. Watch their hands: where do they put them when they speak or when they are quiet, what do they touch and how often and when, how do they shake hands, and so on. For an interesting experience, watch someone walking in a group or a crowd and notice whether he or she is a bouncer, a glider, or a swayer. Once you look at a few people walking, you'll know exactly what I mean. If you can, watch yourself in home movies so you can observe your own patterns.

Many people are not even aware of where their body is or what it is doing at any given moment. This lack of awareness can make them seem awkward even when they don't feel awkward, or it can actually *make* them awkward and more accident-prone. In the professions of acting, dancing, athletics, or martial arts, this wouldn't do at all. To help increase movement awareness, some traditions and teachings have introduced various "centering" techniques. The one I present in the next exercise comes from my adoptive Hawaiian family.

The Story of *Piko-Piko*

A long time ago in old Hawaii, before Captain Cook, Hawaiians used to greet each other with the words, *"Pehea ko piko?"* The literal translation is, "How is your navel?" The real meaning was actually much more profound. In addition to the navel, the word *piko* can also refer to the crown of the head or to the genitals. The crown of the head symbolized the connection to one's ancestors, the navel symbolized one's connection to one's current family, and the genitals symbolized the connection to one's descendants. So the question *"Pehea ko piko?"* really meant, "How are your relationships to these parts of your body and to the relationships that they represent?"

Unfortunately, the missionaries didn't like questions that concerned the genitals or the ancestors, so today we are left with the very bland greeting, *"Pehea 'oe?"* or "How are you?"

The essential meaning of *piko* is "center." Because it is associated with relationships, a technique for healing relationships called *piko-piko* evolved in my Hawaiian family and was taught to me. It is basically a technique that involves focused attention and breathing, and I will give several variations of it for use in healing relationships throughout the book. Meanwhile, here is a variation for relaxing the body that covers all the basics:

1. Inhale with your attention on the crown of your head.

2. Exhale with your attention on your navel.

3. Repeat as desired.

I know, I know, this seems almost too simple. But it does work. The variation in the next exercise is even simpler.

A Conscious Movement Exercise

The purpose of this exercise is to help you become more aware of your body while it is in motion and to give you a way to stay centered at the same time:

1. Do *piko-piko* on your navel. That is, begin by breathing with your attention on your navel as you inhale and exhale.

2. Start moving around in your environment, slowly and with complete conscious awareness of every movement and every part of your body that moves.

3. Pay attention to your balance, your sensations, your feelings, and your thoughts.

4. Try directing your attention elsewhere as you move, and notice any differences in how you move, how you feel, and how you think.

5. Repeat this exercise on different occasions in different places. When you are with other people, move normally, but stay centered and aware. Notice any differences in other people's behavior when you are centered and aware of your body in comparison to when you are not.

Sensory Awareness

I would venture to say that most people take for granted that their five senses of touch, taste, smell, hearing, and sight are giving them a direct experience of the world around them. It may come as a shock to learn, therefore, that such an assumption is a fantasy.

It is true that our sensing organs receive information, but then they convert it into an electrical signal that travels along the pathways of our nervous system by means of neurons, or nerve cells. The information, whatever it is, is passed along from one nerve cell to another, but not directly. Between each nerve cell is a small gap where the information is converted into a different form and handed over to tiny molecules called *neurotransmitters*. These neurotransmitters carry the information across the gap, convert it again, and pass it on to the next nerve cell. Eventually the information reaches its destination where, if the information is important enough, it is mysteriously converted from whatever it has become into what we call *awareness*.

The point is that a great number of little bits of your body are involved in any information received from your skin, your tongue, your nose, your ears, and your eyes. In addition, the information can be distorted at any point along the way, due to tension states, toxins in the body, memory associations, and other things. That's one reason why different people can process the same information and come to very different conclusions about what they are sensing and what it means. The situation is similar to the president of a country trying to find out what's going on in the world when the information he or she gets has been filtered through a billion or more committees. It really is a miracle that we can function at all on this planet, or that we can communicate as well as we do with other people. Nevertheless, given that we receive information the way we do, we may as well learn how to increase the amount of it in order to become more effective at relating to other people—who, after all, have to receive information the same way.

The Sense of Touch

Your sense of touch operates through your skin, and your skin is your largest sensory organ. It's actually your largest organ of any kind, taking up about 16 percent of your whole body mass. I'm not going to go into much detail about how your skin functions, but three things about it are important in terms of relationships:

- Your skin is your most immediate and direct means of contact with other people and the rest of the world.

- It is packed with nerve cells that send messages directly (more or less) to your brain.

- Around the nerves and the hairs on your skin is a lot of muscle tissue that tightens up under physical, emotional, and mental stress, an important result being a diminishing of your sensitivity to and awareness of any information related to your sense of touch.

The phenomenon of being "out of touch" with people is based on the actual effect of skin tension being high enough to block awareness of sensory input. I have worked with people who had suffered from sexual, physical, emotional, or mental abuse. In a number of cases not only did these people have a diminished awareness of touch, but also their skin had a drum-like tightness that made any skin-related sensory input painful. For some of them, even directing conscious attention to their own skin was too much to bear. As we used various means to relieve their skin tension—means that mainly had to do with changing their thinking patterns about other people—their tolerance for touch increased, and their relationships with people improved.

Your sense of touch is not limited to physical contact with someone or something, although tense skin will also limit the amount of information you can get from that source.

Your skin is sensitive as well to air pressure, temperature, electromagnetic fields, light, and what some people call "subtle energy," which can come from electromagnetic or bioenergetic fields. The most sensitive areas of your body are your tongue, lips, face, neck, hands, fingertips, and feet. The part of your body that is least sensitive to touch is the middle of your back.

Normally, touching the skin has a great many more benefits beyond mere sensation. Research shows that children who are touched a lot develop stronger immune systems, grow more quickly, are more emotionally stable, are more alert and active, sleep more soundly, develop movement earlier, and have larger brains than those who receive little or no touch. Studies with adults demonstrate that massage releases endorphins, natural chemicals in the body that ease pain and produce a feeling of well-being. Other studies suggest that people can even learn to distinguish colors through their skin and project a healing influence to others.

Tense skin, however, can inhibit all of these benefits. While the services of a professional masseur or masseuse would be helpful—and the hug or caress of a friend or lover even — better—you don't have to wait for the right occasion, because you can touch yourself and still get most of the benefits.

A Simple Self-Touch Exercise. This exercise is probably best done on bare skin, but your skin will still feel touched even if you do it over clothing.

1. Be as daring or as modest as you choose, and give your skin a light brushing with your hands. At the very least,

include your entire head; your neck and shoulders; your stomach and whatever part of your back you can reach; and your hips, legs, and feet.

2. Give an individual squeeze to each and every finger and toe.

3. Using two or three fingers of either hand, touch and vibrate the skin over the center of your chest, the area on your hands where your thumb and forefinger meet, and on the little bone that sticks out at the top of your spine.

You can practice this exercise as frequently as you like, even partially, to help yourself relax, calm down, and prepare to better enjoy the company of others.

The Sense of Taste

Although wonderful in and of itself, this sense has little to do with relationships, except in certain intimate situations or when you don't like the taste of what a host has served you. Also, about 80 percent of what we taste is due to our perception of how it smells. Therefore, I'm going to pass on further discussion of this sense.

The Sense of Smell

Your sense of smell plays an extremely important role in your relationships, because when you smell someone's odor you are actually taking a piece of that person's body into your own and analyzing the smell itself as well as how it makes you feel.

That's right. As disgusting as it might sound, we detect odors by inhaling airborne bits of things that smell all the way to the back of our noses, where the molecules involved settle into special nerve cells. At that point, as with all our senses, the information about the molecules gets transformed into an electrical signal and starts the familiar neuron-synapse-neuron process toward the brain, but what happens there is anyone's guess. Relatively little research has been done on the physiology of smell, since sight and sound took over as the most important senses of "civilized" people in the nineteenth century. For instance, science writers often say that humans are capable of detecting ten thousand different odors, but that figure is a wild guess (technically called an *assumption*) made by some scientists without any research to back it up. What is known is that professional "noses" (people who smell perfumes and wines for a living) are supposed to be able to distinguish three thousand different odors before graduating from special schools.

More is known about the sense of smell and human behavior, and in this section we'll concentrate on how that affects relationships. But first, a few words about how important the sense of smell is in some cultures around the world:

The Serer tribe in Senegal associates personal identity with odor, believing in two forces defined by scent: a physical one related to the body and the odor of breath; and a spiritual odor that reincarnates in a descendant. Indeed, they claim to be able to recognize a reincarnated ancestor by the smell of a child.

Among the Desana of the Amazon, it is believed that all members of a tribe have a similar odor, and marriages are allowed only between people who smell different.

Instead of anything that we would call perfume, the Dassantch of Ethiopia think that nothing smells better than cows, so as a sign of social status and to attract members of the opposite sex, the men smear themselves with manure and the women cover their upper bodies with butter.

For the Ongee people of the Andaman Islands in the Bay of Bengal off the coast of India, everything in the universe is defined by smell, including personal identity. An Ongee refers to himself by touching the tip of his nose to indicate both "me" and "my odor." Instead of saying, "How are you?" he would say, "How is your nose?"

The Hawaiian language has sixty-four words related to smell in the current dictionary, and there may have been more in the distant past. A traditional greeting still used today is the *honi*, usually described as "to touch noses on the side as a greeting." However, *honi* also means "to smell" or "to sniff," and every traditional Hawaiian with whom I have exchanged this greeting makes sure that sniffing is part of the process. At some point in time there were undoubtedly criteria for determining the character or origin of whomever you were sniffing. It is also known that ancient Hawaiians went out of their way to scent their clothing and bedding with pleasant, natural perfumes and considered some fragrances as food for the gods.

Modern Western Society and Smell. Let's start with dispelling some myths. Men, take note: studies show that most women definitely do not like the smell of male sweat, especially if it's been hanging on his body for more than a few minutes. Women, take note: studies also show that most men couldn't care less about what perfume you are wearing, no matter how expensive it is, unless it is too strong or just smells bad to them. Individual men will have their preferences, of course, and men who specialize in seduction will go out of their way to learn how to identify all the most popular scents by name and manufacturer.

Oh, yes, one of the biggest myths is that if you just dab on a perfume with the right kind of pheromone in it you can make the opposite sex go crazy over you. Pheromones are chemicals emitted by some animals, including insects, specifically for the purpose of sexual attraction. In mammals, these unscented chemicals are perceived by special glands in the nose that are unrelated to smell receptors. Despite marketing claims, current research finds that scientists are not even sure these glands are functional in human beings and do not know how they would function if they *were* active.

Even though the sense of smell is underrated and under-utilized in modern society (not counting the cosmetics industry), the ability to distinguish odors in modern people has not atrophied. Experiments show that both men and women are able to recognize their own spouses and children by scent, even by the scent of their clothes.

Some Simple Practices with Smell. Here are a few things that will help you enhance your sense of smell:

1. It is well known by "noses" and trackers, among others, that the more attention you pay to odors, the greater the number of odors you are able to identify. If you want to increase this ability in order to enhance your relationships, practice smelling your own body and your own clothes, then extend your practice to other people. Sniffing others is considered rather impolite in modern society, so just inhale gently when you are near them.

2. Other experiments show that men and women who wear scents they like experience mood improvements in ways that have a positive effect on their relationships. This strongly suggests that wearing a perfume or cologne that is one of your own favorites may be much better for your relationships than wearing one you think someone else might like.

3. Don't forget the basics. Clean bodies are generally nicer to associate with, scented or unscented.

The Sense of Hearing

So much about the human body is miraculous, and right near the top of the list is our sense of hearing. With a sense organ about the size of a pea we are able to locate, distinguish, and process sounds that come from different sources and vibrate at different frequencies. What's more, this organ is able to take responsibility for our sense of balance at the same time.

The way it works is almost unbelievable. Sound waves come through the air and hit your outer ear (the part that some of you wish were smaller and some of you wish were closer to your head). The outer ear channels the sound waves into the inner ear, where they cause your eardrum to vibrate. This causes a hammer bone to hit an anvil bone that hits a stirrup bone that hits another type of drum that causes waves in a liquid to move little hairs that change the vibrational information to electrical signals that hop and skip their way to the brain. And without even thinking, you are able to instantly tell the difference between a whisper and thunder.

Such sound waves are not a direct experience of the source of sound, however. When you speak to another person, you vibrate your larynx and manipulate your mouth, tongue, and lips in such a way as to send modulated waves through the air, hoping that the other person's sound-receiver system can interpret the information carried by those waves in the way you want them to.

More than any other sense, your sense of hearing is dependent on your mental concentration. If you stop concentrating on a particular sound, it can disappear completely from your conscious awareness, even when it is quite loud.

Sometimes this disappearance is a good thing. When my wife and I lived in Senegal we had a villa on a peninsula called "La Corniche." We were happy there until we discovered that our home was directly in line with the last landing phase of the passenger jets coming into the Dakar Airport. At times it sounded, and felt, as if the wheels of the planes were rolling on our roof. I don't recall how long it took for us to get used to it, but I do remember having guests one night and being surprised during a conversation at the sudden, startled look on their faces as they stared upward. It took a conscious effort to bring the jet noise back into my awareness so that I could sympathize with them.

Sometimes the ability to screen out sounds is not such a good thing, such as when you are talking to an important, but boring, person and your attention drifts away while they are saying something they believe is significant.

Being able to hear what a person is actually saying, rather than what you think they *might* be saying, can make or break a relationship. Because we have this ability to tune out as well as to tune in sounds, it frequently happens that two people speaking to each other are each having a one-way conversation. Here are two exercises to help you improve your ability to tune in at will:

Concentrated Hearing: Exercise One. The purpose of this exercise is to help you experience the effect of shifting your attention while listening to one source of sound.

1. Pick out some music you like and play it. Just listen to it as you normally would for about thirty seconds.

2. While the music is playing, maintain your awareness of it and simultaneously put your attention in the center of your head. Do this for about thirty seconds and see how that feels.

3. In the same way, shift your attention for thirty seconds at a time to the center of your chest, your stomach, your hands, and your ears.

4. The next time you have an extended conversation with someone, try the same exercise and experience the effect.

Concentrated Hearing: Exercise Two. The purpose of this exercise is to help you expand your awareness of more than one sound at a time. For instance, as I'm writing this I am aware of the sound of my computer keys, the sound of my noisy computer itself, the sound of a neighbor mowing his lawn, and the sound of my tendons rubbing over my bones as I turn my head.

1. In whatever your environment at the moment, focus your attention on hearing itself: how many different sounds can you hear around (and inside) you?

2. Practice with a particular type of sound—such as wind, water, or traffic—and count how many different sounds you can hear within the main source. You might be surprised.

The Sense of Sight

Did you know that you are not really looking at anything you are seeing? That's a fact of life, and there isn't anything you can do about it, because your sense of sight comes from the ability of your eyes to perceive reflected light. In actuality, what you see when you look at a friend or a lover is only whatever frequency ranges of light energy are not being absorbed by that person's body or clothing. If people didn't reflect any light, they would appear either pitch black (if they absorbed all the light energy) or invisible (if they let it all pass through them). Reflected light is at best an indirect way of seeing anyone or anything, but it's all we have.

Of course, it's not that simple. Light rays don't just go right through your eyes to your brain. There is ample room for distortion before you become aware of what or whom you see.

The process of seeing begins as light enters your eye's *cornea*, a rather thick, protective, and transparent layer of cells that covers your whole eye. Then the light passes through your *pupil*, the dark hole in the center of your eye adjusted in size by the colored muscle called the *iris*. Next, the light moves on through a lens, passes through a jelly-like substance, and finally reaches the back of the eye to land on a surface called the *retina*. Science writers love to tell you that the image you are receiving is projected onto the retina upside down—as on a movie screen—but this is totally misleading. The retina is made up of millions of light-sensitive cells divided into two types, called *rods* and *cones*. The rods help you to recognize shapes, and they work best in dim lighting. The cones help you to recognize colors, and they work best in bright light. Both types of cells combine their information, convert it into electrical signals, and send it through the optic-nerve system to the brain, which then does its mysterious thing so that you can see. Even more mysteriously, according to recent research there are enormous variations in the distribution of color-sensitive cone cells among people, yet remarkably similar experiences of color. And that's the *simple* explanation.

Distortion of information received from a light source can occur in many different ways. There are numerous muscles in and around the eye, and the tenser those muscles are, the harder it is for people to see clearly. This can make a big difference in how well a relationship functions, especially if you can't tell whether a person is happy or sad, not to mention the other more subtle, visual signs of emotion that people convey, consciously and subconsciously. For instance, my wife tells me that one side of my nose twitches very slightly when I don't want to do something. Similarly, when *she* doesn't want to do something, I notice a "look," a particular, indefinable expression on her face. If our vision weren't clear enough, we would miss out on all those little signs.

A Simple Exercise to Ease Eye Tension. This exercise can provide temporary or permanent eye-tension relief, depending on how much and how often you do it. After my father-in-law did it extensively for three months, he threw away his glasses at age fifty and never wore or needed glasses again, even though he lived to be ninety-one. I use the exercise occasionally when I need to read the fine print on a vitamin bottle. If your eyes are tense for emotional rather than physical reasons, it will provide temporary relief only.

1. Squeeze your eyes shut five times in a row.
2. Look at something and try to feel or imagine that your pupil is expanding.
3. Repeat as desired.

A very different kind of visual distortion can occur because of your brain's ability to make up things. I'm not talking about mental fantasies; I'm talking about *hallucination*, the apparent experience of sensory input that isn't really there in the outer world. Your brain hallucinates all the time and has the ability to do so because of an oddity in the way mammalian eyes are constructed. Remember the optic nerve mentioned above? Well, instead of being nicely positioned off to the side, as it is in octopus eyes, in mammals it is attached directly to the retina, displacing a certain number of rods and cones. As a result, everyone— and that means *everyone*—has a literal blind spot in each eye, a place where light isn't registered at all. Without some form of compensation, we would all "see" a black hole from each eye as we look around, which obviously would be very inconvenient. So the brain compensates by creating the illusion that we can see something when we really can't.

How to Find Your Blind Spot. There are a number of different ways to demonstrate how to find your blind spot, but I've chosen the most portable one.

1. Stand or sit, and find an object straight ahead of you at eye level to look at that is farther away than the length of your arm.

2. Look at this object, extend your left arm out and raise your thumb in front of the object at about the level of your nose, and close your right eye.

3. Keeping your left eye on the object, slowly move your thumb horizontally to the left until the top of your thumb disappears. This is your physical blind spot. You can do the same thing with your left eye and your right thumb. The exact location of this spot will vary with individuals.

If this exercise sounds too complicated, you can use the image below to experience the same effect:

Hold the above image about 20 inches or 50 centimeters away from you and close your right eye. Look at the plus sign with your left eye and slowly bring the image closer. When it reaches a certain distance, the dot will disappear because it has reached the blind spot on your retina. Try it the other way by closing your left eye, looking at the dot with your right eye, and bringing the image closer until the plus sign disappears.

The reason you do not see this blind spot when you look around is that your brain fills in the blank area with information from the other data within your range of vision, thus making it seem as if your eyes are seeing the whole picture.

Your brain uses this ability in other situations as well. Speaking metaphorically, in English we say that someone has a "blind spot" when that person sees some life experience, not as everyone else does, but only as they think it ought to be. Various psycho-physiological experiments have demonstrated the literal capacity of the brain to change data to fit expectations. In one such experiment, subjects saw and recorded black aces of spades and red eights of hearts projected onto a movie screen, when the actual projection was of red aces of spades and black eights of hearts. In another experiment, a man was fitted with special glasses that turned the world upside down to his sight. He wore them night and day, and on the third day, in spite of the glasses, his brain turned the world right side up again.

In dealing with other people, we sometimes project our expectations onto them without really seeing who they are. Parents may see their adult progeny as the little children they once were, instead of who they have become. Women who have been hurt by men, and men who have been hurt by women, may see all members of the opposite sex as replicas of the one who hurt them. Judges may see criminals as potentially good citizens, no matter how terrible their crimes. And people may see stereotypes of race or religion, instead of individual human beings. I remember talking about this with a fellow sergeant in the United States Marine Corps. The man was upset and confused because his personal experience of "blacks" (the appropriate term current at the time for people of African descent) in our unit was good, but his learned experience handed down through his family was that they were bad. It is the brain that creates these experiences, fed by fear, desire, and—naturally—sensory information.

A Technique for Clearing Unwanted Hallucinations. This technique will only work if you really want to see through the fog of any expectations you have. It will not get rid of expectations; it will simply give you another perception.

1. Start by deciding to act as if, for any period of time you decide on, that this is your very first day on Earth. The only knowledge you have is how to speak the languages you've learned. Most especially, pretend you have no memories associated with any other human being except, perhaps, of what their relationship is to you. That relationship, however, is what it is only in the present moment and has no history.

2. Encounter or think about a person currently in your life. If the person is present, speak to him or her and observe behavior, but do not refer to anything in the past or in the future, because, for now, that information is not available. For the same reason, do not compare that person to anyone else, not even to a vision of what he or she could be, and especially not to what he or she might have done in the past, because the past does not exist while this technique is being used. If the person is not present, just remember his or her behavior without trying to interpret it, as if you were an anthropologist doing raw research.

3. Pay attention to your feelings while doing this exercise and to how easy or difficult it seems. Most of all, see if you can learn anything you did not know before.

Chapter 5

Your Relationship with Your Mind

Iow can you have a relationship with something as insubstantial as the mind? Most people in the scientific community do not even like to admit that there is such a thing as the mind. Their idea of the "mind/body" connection is that the mind is an effect of the body, the brain in particular. Even so, they have no idea how a physical experience, like sensation, can become a mental experience, or how a thought can transform itself into a physical effect.

Most people know that, even though the state of the body can affect the mind and the state of the mind can affect the body, large and important types of experience are not physical at all. Imagination and fantasy, recall and expectations, speculation and reasoning—the list can go on and on; nevertheless, the mind remains difficult to define. *Webster's Encyclopedic Unabridged Dictionary of the English Language* defines mind as "that part of a man which thinks, feels, and wills." Not bad, but the word *think* is still pretty vague, even in this comprehensive dictionary, because it is used to cover so many different things. And then there's the problem with the act of thinking itself. We think thoughts. We think about thoughts. We think thoughts about things, and we think about the thoughts that we have about things. We also think about thinking. This approach isn't going to lead us to anything useful.

I'm going to cut through such problems with a radically different definition of the mind and the phenomenon of thinking. First, though, I'm going to define the body as the part of human beings that senses, remembers, and moves. That brings us to my definition of the mind: the part of human beings that perceives, recalls, and imagines. The act of thinking, by this definition, is simply the act of perceiving, recalling, and imagining.

Even as I write these words, I can mentally hear the objections—or am I just imagining them? Anyway, let me explain first why I chose this definition and then how it will help you establish a better relationship with your own mind, which will in turn help you with your other relationships, too.

The Perceiving Mind

The body senses and the mind perceives. What's the difference? In the current context, sensing is the purely physical operation of receiving information through the sensory organs, converting that information into electrical signals, passing the converted information on to the brain and/or other parts of the body, and storing the information in some manner (we are not going to discuss the storage system in this book). In contrast, perceiving is the purely mental operation of becoming aware of information, whether it comes from your sensory organs or any other source. This perception might take the form of visual, auditory, kinesthetic, or other kinds of awareness.

An Exercise in Perception

This exercise is designed to help you perceive things in a slightly different way, with the idea that, eventually, it will help you to perceive *people* in a slightly different way.

1. Touch as many things as you can within your reach. Be aware of differences in texture and temperature.

2. Listen to all the sounds around you. Be aware of differences in pitch (highness or lowness), loudness, and quality (a computer sounds different than a fan, which sounds different than a bird).

3. Look at the different shapes of things, at the spaces between objects, and at their colors. Try to find all the colors of the rainbow, plus white and black.

Perceptual Frameworks

As I said above, perceiving is not the same as sensing, because perception involves interpretation of what we are sensing. Interpretation is always based on rules, which will be discussed later, and most often on "rule sets" or frameworks of which we are seldom consciously aware.

For instance, you may perceive some people from within the framework of being a customer or a client, an employee or an employer, a student or a teacher—and your relationships with them will be modified by this perception. Furthermore, your general perspective will also affect what and how much of your sensory environment you perceive. If you are not sure about that last part, try this experiment:

1. Wherever you are, look around your environment as if you were a photographer. Be aware of what you see and how you see it.

2. In the same way, look at your environment as if you were a landscape artist (outdoors) or an interior designer (indoors).

3. Now look around outdoors as if you were a farmer, or indoors as if you were a carpenter.

If you pay close attention, you will notice that each change in your perceptual framework makes certain things important and other things unimportant. As you change frameworks, some things draw your attention and others fade into the background or out of your perception entirely. The same thing happens when we perceive people within different frameworks. The narrower the framework—such as that of a stereotype—the less we perceive who is actually there.

Extended Perception

Another kind of perception receives information from sources other than the ordinary senses as we usually think of them. You may prefer to call this kind of perception "intuition" or "hunches," but the fact remains that we often perceive information about other people that cannot be explained by conventional ideas about physiology and consciousness. This book will not go into where such information might originate. Suffice it to say that this kind of perception plays an important role in all relationships. Sometimes it takes the form of mental imagery, sometimes what can be called *mental sound*, and sometimes a peculiar sense of "knowing." Often it takes the form of an unexplainable "feeling" that may be pleasant or unpleasant, attractive or repelling. Any such perception may influence either our reactions or our actions in regard to other people, so they ought to be taken into account.

THE RECALLING MIND

Let me begin by making an important distinction between remembering and recalling. By my definition, it is the body that remembers, literally, and the mind that recalls.

As needed, or stimulated, the body puts together scattered records of sensory experience and reenacts them in the present moment. Sometimes this act of remembering involves the mind, but often it does not. There are many physical and emotional actions, reactions, and habits in which people engage without thinking about them. You may smile automatically when you see someone you like or frown without even realizing it when you hear the voice of someone you don't like. Your body may drive your car for you while you converse with a friend; and under certain circumstances you may laugh or cry without intending to, because your body has reacted to something it has smelled or heard or seen that is below the level of your conscious perception.

Recall, in contrast to remembering, is a function of the mind. A lot of our thinking time is taken up with recalling events and experiences. For instance, you may purposely recall a list of tasks that you are supposed to do, bring experiences back into awareness when you look at a photograph or watch a home movie, call up the words and music of a song you want to sing to someone, or spontaneously think of a long-past event when you smell a particular odor.

Your ability to recall is most evident when you recognize things, like people's faces and voices. It is also very evident when you speak to someone, because in the act of speaking you are recalling not only how to speak but also the grammar and vocabulary you need to express what you want to say.

Typically, when you recall an event, like a party, you first think of the specific happening that made the most impression on you, emotionally or physically. Maybe you first recall the eyes of a nice person you met, or the drink someone spilled on you, or a particular piece of music. The longer you keep your attention on the party, the more specific happenings you recall, until, in assorted order, you recall pretty much the whole event. Your mind also has the ability to impose chronological order on the recall, but that takes more concentration. Just as with any talent, the more you practice detailed recall, the better you get at it and the more able you are to bring back into conscious awareness other talents and skills, as well as information.

An Exercise in Recall

This is the type of exercise you can do to gain the benefits mentioned above. Use the suggestions given here, or do it your way. The more time you give each recall, the more details will come forth.

1. Recall the first pretty girl or handsome boy you ever saw, or the earliest one you can. What did he or she really look like? Hair color? Eye color? Clothing? Movement? Voice? Location?

2. Recall your first kiss. Who was it with? How did it feel? Were the other person's lips warm or cool? Was it just a kiss, or was there touching, too? Was it daytime or nighttime? Did you like or not?

3. Recall the best dinner out you ever had with someone. Where was it? What did you eat and drink? How did it taste? What was the server like? Was there any music? Who paid the bill?

PATTERN RECOGNITION

As I discussed in chapter 4, the phenomenon of the hole in your vision and how your brain fills it in has far-reaching consequences for many things in your life, including your relationships. Recognizing someone's face comes from the stimulation of a remembered pattern of shape and color and, sometimes, movement. When we have the experience of recognizing someone from behind at a distance, it can occur with only the stimulation of part of a remembered pattern. Your brain fills in the rest, and because of that filling in, the recognition may not always be correct. In the same way, the sight or sound or smell or touch of a person may stimulate your recall of only part of a remembered pattern associated with that person. You may or may not find it useful that your brain fills in the rest of the pattern. It's like some of the new word-processing programs that fill in a word for you when you type in the first one or two letters. Sometimes that saves you time, and sometimes it wastes your time, because it isn't what you want and you have to stop and correct the mistake.

As a young man I sometimes went to restaurants where the waitresses prided themselves on recalling what kind of drink and meal the customer wanted. Serving me upset them, because I wanted something different every time. Even greater problems can occur when your expectations of a person's behavior, based on filled-in pattern recall, no longer match who that person has become. We'll cover that in another chapter, however. For now, I would like to give you an experience that demonstrates how your brain fills in patterns for you to fit remembered patterns.

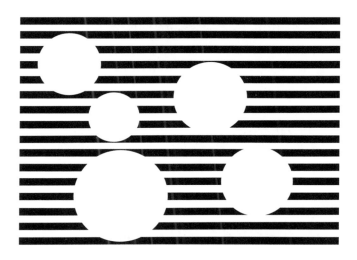

When you look at this drawing, what do you see? Chances are that you say you see five white circles in the midst of black-and-white lines. However, the appearance of the circles is in fact an illusion. The drawing consists only of broken lines; it is your brain that gives you the images of circles where there aren't any. The same process occurs when you see faces in clouds, or rocks, or carpets. Actually, the same process occurs when you watch cartoons or look at impressionist paintings. It happens again when you look at images of people formed out of lots of really tiny photographs, called "photo mosaics," or see images in the computer-generated dots of stereograms. And it happens in some way or another with all of the people whom you meet and know.

CHAPTER 5

THE IMAGINING MIND

The imagining part of the mind is the operation that has the greatest influence on relationships. This part of my discussion may evoke the most controversy, since I have a very different view of what constitutes imagination than do many theorists.

In the following paragraphs, I will discuss various mental activities that I consider to fall within the province of imagination.

Reasoning

The ability to reason is often thought of as the grandest of human attributes, something that sets us apart from the other animals, including our disturbingly close relatives, the chimpanzees. Cicero put it this way:

> Wise men are instructed by reason;
> men of less understanding, by experience;
> the most ignorant, by necessity;
> and beasts by nature.

That idea sounds very noble, but what does it really mean? Reasoning is usually defined as the ability to draw logical conclusions from a truth, and therein lies its weakness. The validity of the logic is entirely dependent on what is defined as truth. If a given group of people were to hold it as true that men were superior to women by their very nature, then reason would dictate that men should receive more benefits and privileges than women, no matter how competent the women might be. If, in the same way, another group were to believe without a doubt that what it believes is the only possible truth, then reason would dictate that all other beliefs are false and should be ignored or suppressed.

The question before us is, *where does truth come from?* The answer is, *from people.* Individual people like you and me. Truths don't fall out of the sky. Someone has to make them up.

That's right. Someone makes them up. Do you recall what I said about rules in the first chapter? Here is how a truth is created:

- You have an experience.

- You make up a rule about what the experience means, usually based on recall of similar experiences or recall of what someone else has told you.

- At this point, if you are unsure about the meaning, you call it an opinion. If you don't doubt it, you call it a truth.

- The rule you made up about the meaning of the experience is remembered by your body and available for recall.

- Frequently recalled opinion rules often become rules of truth.

Just to make it clear, I'm saying that the whole process of reasoning begins with rules (some people call them assumptions) that you or someone else has made up about an experience of some kind. That is, the ability to reason is based on imagination.

Why is this so important to know? Because everything you believe about anything is based on made-up rules. All your beliefs about yourself—about relationships; about men, women, children; about all the individuals you know—are really rules. More importantly, the rules you have about these things affect your experience with them. If your rules are affecting your relationships in a good way, that's great. If not, there's good news and bad news. The good news is that rules can be changed. The bad news is that they may be hard to change unless you know what they are.

Actually, that's not really bad news, because I'm going to help you discover what your rules are, so that you can change them if you wish. First, I'm going to ask you to make a short list—not more than four items to begin with—of beliefs that you think you have about yourself in relation to other people, or that you would like to have. The technique I'm about to give will help you discover if what you *think* you believe is what you *really* believe. You'll know the difference by your reactions to the technique. It can also help you to reinforce beliefs you already have or replace old beliefs with new ones. You can choose any belief you want to work with, but here's a sample list to get you started:

- I love myself
- People like me
- I like people
- I am attractive

Now, here's the technique:

1. Set two small bowls in front of you, side by side.

2. In one of the bowls, place twenty-five to fifty small objects, such as beads, coins, or marbles.

3. One at a time, move an object from one bowl to the other. Each time you move an object, state a belief or a rule of your choice. Use the same statement throughout the session.

4. Continue the process, making the statement and moving the objects back and forth between the bowls for as long as you like.

There is no way to predict what effect this exercise will have for a particular person. If the belief you state corresponds closely with what your body remembers and feels, you may not experience much of anything. If your statement represents an idea that you like, and if it's not opposed by any strong memories, then you may feel a rising sense of excitement. But if, on the other hand, the statement is in sharp opposition to your established rules or beliefs, then your experience could include unpleasant physical, emotional, or even mental reactions. It is not uncommon for a feeling of tension or anxiety to occur in the chest area, but there could be other reactions, too. This result is only a sign that opposing ideas exist. You can choose either to stop and put the bowls and objects away or to keep strengthening the idea you like by using the technique frequently until the new rule has become a truth for you.

Decision Making

What do decisions have to do with imagination? Everything. Making decisions is usually considered to be a purely intellectual activity, sometimes influenced by emotions and sometimes guided by cold logic. I hate to burst anyone's bubble, but decisions are clearly based on imagination (see the next chapter); and "cold logic," as we have seen above, begins with imagination.

We make decisions in the first place because we imagine that something is going to happen and then we imagine the best way to deal with it. If you decide to write a book, for instance, it is only because you have already imagined doing, saying, or receiving something as a result that feels good to you. Then you imagine the best way to write the book, and then you do it.

Many people try to separate the activities of thinking about something, deciding to do something, and doing something, but in my view they are all part of the same process. Thinking about something—which is the same as imagining doing it—may stir up feelings, but unless it switches on a habit or leads to the next step, no action will be taken. Deciding to do the thing—which is the same as imagining the act of doing it in a concentrated way—will automatically lead to the doing if nothing else happens to inhibit it. And the only thing that *could* inhibit it is a decision *not* to do it.

Your body always responds to your mind. Think a thought and your body immediately begins to act it out in whatever way it can. If you have established a habit (a remembered rule or set of rules) that tells your body not to fully act out what you think, then your body will act it out in a partial way. You may have a mean boss and think about kicking him or her, but you may also have remembered rules that say, "No, no, no! Kicking is bad or dangerous! Do not do that!" In this case, your body will immediately start to act out the thought of kicking your boss, getting all the muscles ready to do the job, and just as immediately stop the action by increasing tension in those muscles so that the act cannot be carried out. The more strongly you feel about the act, the more tension the body needs to generate in order to stop it. Mentally, what has happened is that you have imagined doing something and then quickly imagined *not* doing it.

Most people I have met or taught think of imagination as some long, drawn-out process, and sometimes it is. Sometimes, though, it happens so quickly that you don't consciously notice it. The next exercise will help you notice it more often.

An Exercise in Decision Making. Every physical action you perform, and every emotional reaction you feel, is preceded by a decision. And every decision is an act of imagination that stimulates your body into physical action or emotional reaction. If you think this has nothing to do with relationships, you aren't thinking. Try this exercise:

1. Decide to pick up something, and pick it up. Pay very close attention to what you are thinking as you make the decision.

2. Decide to pick up, and then pick up, several things until you can really be aware of what your mind is doing when you make the decision.

3. Decide to pick up something, and then do not pick it up. Pay very close attention to what you are thinking as you make both decisions.

4. Repeat this process with several objects until you can really be aware of what your mind is doing when you make the decisions.

Concentration

Also called *focus*, concentration is the ability to center your attention on something to the exclusion of other stimuli. Imagination is the source of this ability, because first you imagine focusing on something, and then you perceive the information your senses give you in that area of attention. Imagination used this way generally happens so quickly you might not notice it, but if you pay attention to the process for a while it will become evident. In the absence of a physical defect or disease, the ability to narrow or to broaden concentration comes from a combination of imagination (to move the attention), recall (about remembered rules concerning what's important and what isn't), and perception (awareness that is restricted or broad, depending on the rules).

An Exercise in Concentration. This exercise will help you to become more aware of the process of changing your focus:

1. Look at an object that is at least ten feet or three meters away from you.

2. Become aware of some detail of that object.

3. Notice how much of what is around it tends to fade out of your perception.

4. Keep your attention centered on the object, but expand your awareness of your peripheral vision.

5. Notice how many other things now come into your perception.

I can concentrate on something, like a good book or a computer game, to the exclusion of practically everything else outside the area of my restricted perception. Unfortunately, this means that sometimes I don't hear my wife calling me for dinner. On the other hand, I do a lot of teaching around the world, and I have found that maintaining peripheral awareness while I teach is extremely useful, so that I can be aware of temperature, lighting, potential disturbances, and audience reactions. Imagination is what guides our concentration and helps us to change our focus from narrow to broad as needed or desired.

Another Exercise in Concentration. The type of image below, known as "Rubin's Vase," was introduced by Danish psychologist Edgar Rubin in 1915. He developed such ambiguous, two-dimensional forms to demonstrate optical illusions. This particular one is quite famous, and I think it demonstrates the effects of shifting focus even better than the exercise above does.

Rubin's Vase

Using your imagination, make the decision to go back and forth between concentrating on the black part of the image and the white part, and notice how your perception changes as a result.

Is it a vase on a black background, or two people on a white background about to kiss? It isn't either one, actually, but as you change your focus from the white part to the black part, your wonderful brain will give an image based on a remembered pattern.

Some people take advantage of this image-making propensity of the brain by using disguises that promote pattern fill-in and so alter expectations. Examples include clothing identified with a particular culture or subculture, eyeglasses or hair color identified with a particular personality type, speech patterns identified with a particular ethnic group or area, and so on. The experts in such disguises know how to make small changes that your brain interprets as big changes. Cosmetics are used in a similar way.

It is astounding how different a celebrity can look with and without make-up.

Analysis

Technically, analysis is the process of studying the nature of something by separating its parts and determining their relationships in order to predict behavior in relation to something else. In the 1950s, the psychiatrist Eric Berne developed a method of applying this process to people called "Transactional Analysis." He defined a transaction as an exchange of communication between people. These exchanges were separated into positive exchanges, called *strokes,* and negative exchanges, called *games,* and analyzed in great detail. The method is still in use and has proven beneficial to many people. As is typical of analytical systems, it can get complicated, because you never run out of things and ways to analyze.

Much earlier, in the 1890s, Sigmund Freud developed a system of psychoanalysis, based on a process of analyzing three factors supposedly common to all people: the Id, the Ego, and the Super-Ego. A lot of people have benefited from that system, too. And in the ancient system of Huna psychology I teach, we analyze the relationships between the *Ku* (body mind), the *Lono* (conscious mind), and the *Kane* (higher self). Needless to say, many people benefit from this system as well.

However, these and all other systems of personality or relationship analysis are based on the *imagined* existence of imagined parts that can be analyzed. Different people at different times have observed human behavior and used their imaginations to divide that behavior arbitrarily into segments to be studied. In reality, there is no Ego, no Ku, and no Transaction, unless you decide to look at human behavior that way. Likewise, there is no month of June, unless you decide to divide the year up into twelve months and call one of them *June*. It is human imagination that divides up the year, not nature. And different human beings divide up things differently. That's why the Gregorian calendar, the Jewish calendar, the Mayan calendar, and the Hawaiian calendar are not the same.

Here's one more example: Today we use a "scientific classification" system for analyzing plants and animals, including humans. Bottle-nosed dolphins are classified as being of the class of Mammals, the order of Cetacea (whales), the suborder of Odontoceti (toothed whales), the family of Delphinidae (all dolphins and close relatives), and the genus and species of *Tursiops truncatus* (specifically, the bottle-nosed dolphin). All of this starts with their classification as Mammals, which means that they share three characteristics with all other mammals: three ear bones, hair (dolphins have it, but not much), and mammary glands. So of course it's easy to tell the difference between a dolphin and a shark, right? Sharks don't have any of those three things, and in addition they breathe with gills, their tails are vertical instead of horizontal, and they don't have a backbone. Nevertheless, at some point someone decided (i.e., imagined) that certain characteristics about dolphins were more important than other characteristics. And from that initial assumption an extremely logical system for analyzing the place of dolphins in zoology came about. In different times, under different circumstances, the ancient Hawaiians saw dolphins differently. Their system was far less complicated, but, based on what they imagined was important, they classified dolphins with sharks. After all, both dolphins and sharks have vertical dorsal fins; both have teeth, give birth to live young, gather in groups, surf, etc. Our modern classification system is the most popular one, but that doesn't mean that it's the only possible one.

My point here is that even an intellectual process like analysis is based on imagination. First you imagine that certain characteristics about something are important. Then you invent a classification system based on those characteristics. Then you observe members of the system you have invented and use your imagination further to restrict your analysis to behavior that fits the system. And oh, by the way, what's your astrological sign? Or your Chinese year? Or your Jungian archetype? Or your ethnic origin? Or your Ayurvedic body type? Or your Enneagram number? Or your age?

An Experience with Analysis. Even though it starts with imagination, analysis can be useful.

1. Divide your behavior into good behavior and bad behavior. You will have to invent or imagine a means of determining which is which.

2. Analyze the amount of time devoted to each type of behavior during a typical day.

3. Imagine what that means or what you can do with that information.

119

Planning

When you plan anything—whether a speech, a party, or a spiritual revolution—the role of imagination is obvious. First you imagine what you want, and then you imagine the steps or the actions it will take to get it. Writing a plan down does not make it more real. The writing (or drawing) is just a representation of the plan. The plan itself is still only in your mind until you execute it. While you are executing it, the plan is in your perception. Then it becomes a memory and is available for recall.

In terms of your personal development, one of the most useful types of planning is called *rehearsal*. In it, you imagine doing something as vividly as you can, using all your senses. This helps to establish memory patterns that can come into play when the event you are planning actually occurs. You can rehearse as a purely mental activity, of course, knowing that your body will be involved automatically to the extent that your imagined sensory experience is vivid enough; but you can more easily access the memory patterns when you engage physically in the rehearsal, even in a small way.

During certain periods of my life I was an amateur actor in different groups. Sometimes we would have to use a small room for rehearsals because the theater wasn't available. Using vivid imagination, we had to make three steps represent ten steps, and often we had to react physically to imagined props and furniture. At the same time, we had to keep in mind our imagined audience, so that we could maintain our proper position in relation to it. At other times, we would rehearse in one type of location only to discover that the final location for the play was completely different. That taught us flexibility, because plans—being imaginary events—don't always work out the same as the event itself.

Another thing that taught us flexibility was the fact that when it came time to execute the plan, not everyone would remember it—usually in the form of forgetting lines, not responding to a cue, or misinterpreting a cue. As a member of the Dakar Dramatic Society in Senegal, I was once in a play called *Hello Out There*, by William Saroyan. It was about a young man traveling through West Texas who was framed for a crime he didn't commit and put in jail. I played the young man, and friends from the American, British, and Canadian embassies played the other characters. On one particular evening, the little dinner theater where we were performing was filled with men and women who actually were from West Texas. They were part of an oil exploration team, and some of them had never been to a play before, so they were somewhat rowdy and talkative during the performance.

Near the middle of the play was my big moment, a long monologue during which I would be the only one on the stage.

Before that could happen, however, one of the characters—my secretary in real life—was supposed to come to my cell door and tell me that she was going to go out and see if anyone else was in the jailhouse. Her exit is what would leave me alone to give my speech. But the rowdy audience had shaken her confidence. Unfortunately, when she approached my cell, she jeopardized my stellar performance by giving me the line that she wasn't supposed to say until *after* she had come back from checking the jailhouse.

"There's no one there," she said.

I wasn't about to give up my monologue, so I said, "Go and see anyway."

"But there's no one there," she insisted.

This exchange went on a couple more times. Finally, I reached through the bars, grabbed her by the shoulders, pulled her right up to my face, and said firmly, "Please, go out and check again! Right now!" An additional little shake brought her memory back. At last she left, and the stage was mine.

We can learn several useful things from this anecdote. First, thanks to rehearsal we both knew what to do when the event was in progress. My secretary needed a little reminding, but once back on track she followed the rehearsed pattern of behavior. Second, plans don't happen automatically; they happen because people carry them out. My motivation was to complete my part of the plan that made the play successful. Without that, the play, the plan, would have fallen apart. Third, no plan is perfect, because no plan can foresee everything that might happen. Thus, the purpose of the plan is more important than the plan itself. If you remember that, you can more easily change your plan as needed.

Plans have no special power. They are not sacred in any way. They are pure imagination until human beings act to make them happen, and even then a plan ought never to take precedence over the people carrying it out. People don't fail. Plans fail. And plans can be changed.

An Experience with Rehearsal. Regardless of what I've just said, plans—and rehearsal for plans—can be extremely useful for giving a sense of security to your body and confidence to your mind. We'll make use of them in various parts of this book, but for now let's try something simple. This exercise will help you to get used to the process:

1. Think of something you need to do or want to do with someone else. It could be taking someone out for dinner, discussing finances, asking for a favor—anything.

2. In your mind, imagine doing it as clearly and as vividly as you can.

3. When you actually do the thing, pay close attention to how your body feels or reacts and how your mind operates while you are doing it.

Fantasy

Fantasy is what many people think imagination is, because they have been taught that "imagined" is the same as "unreal." You may think it odd, but I agree with that. All of our thoughts are unreal, but only if we define "reality" as information received by our mind through our sensory organs. Based on what we know about our senses, though, that definition is rather humorous. It means that "reality" is a bunch of electrical signals, processed in some mysterious way by our brain so that they are perceived by our mind as sights, sounds, touch, and so on.

Hold on a minute! If I continue in that way I'll find myself forced to assert that everything we experience is a fantasy, and I'd rather not do that. Let's start over and talk about fantasy as being "unreal" experience. Let's go even further and define *fantasy* as "imagined experience that is improbable, highly unlikely, or totally unrelated to ordinary sensory experience." Imagining yourself as Superman, Wonder Woman, or Emperor/Empress of the world would fall into that category, as would a great many other imagined experiences.

Besides being a wonderful resource for novels, movies, and a multitude of emotionally satisfying adventures, fantasy also has a very practical personal use.

I've already told you about how your body responds to your thoughts—all your thoughts. When you imagine a sensory experience, your imagining activates all the muscles and nerves that would be activated by an equivalent sensory experience, too. Where fantasy is concerned, this means that, if you fantasize yourself as a superhero, your body immediately starts to modify your muscles, your nerve impulses, and your internal chemistry in ways designed to simulate your fantasy image as closely as possible. The degree of modification depends entirely on the degree of intensity you are able to conjure up, in combination with any inhibitions or restrictions imposed by your remembered rules and your body's actual physical capabilities. At the least, such a fantasy would result in a certain amount of increase in muscle strength and sensory potential, but how much for a particular individual is anybody's guess. Still, it's a cheap workout. But kidding aside, the difference will often be measurable with equipment designed to test muscle strength and sensory perception. One brief fantasy episode may not be enough to register, of course, but with practice you can improve the effect.

No matter how wild or abstract your fantasy is, your body will try its best to respond in an equivalent way. Fantasy can improve your looks, or at least your appeal, and can help to create the kind of personality other people would enjoy being around.

The most powerful experience I ever had in this regard took place during a workshop in which I participated. The format was simple. After a few over-long relaxation meditations, each student in turn had an opportunity to stand on a stage and talk about himself or herself. The facilitator, who was very good and compassionate, would add helpful questions or suggestions. The powerful experience occurred when a young woman, perhaps eighteen or twenty years old, got up to speak. She was blonde and shy and her looks were plain; she had the kind of face you might not even notice in a crowd. As her shyness and low self-esteem became more evident, the facilitator suggested that she repeat the statement, "I am beautiful." She needed some coaxing, and everyone felt sorry for her . . . at first. Even if you believe it isn't true, you can't make a statement like that over and over again without fantasy being stimulated to some degree. The facilitator kept her at it for about five minutes, when suddenly there was a gasp from the audience—especially the men and including me. In my perception, it was as if a wave of some kind had passed over her face, and then she *was* beautiful. That's right, she went from plain to beautiful in five minutes, and she was besieged by men asking her for a date for the rest of the workshop.

Here, I am not suggesting that you live your whole life in a fantasy world that other people don't share, because that could get you into trouble. People who suffer from psychoses are often lost in their own private fantasy worlds. Instead, and as the young woman's story shows, I am talking about the healthy approach to fantasy, which is to use it to enhance your relationships in the same world that everyone else shares. Use your fantasies to help you feel better, and check the effects on your relationships. Then you can use that information to modify your fantasies.

An Experiment with Fantasy. We're going to start with something simple:

1. Imagine yourself taller, slimmer, stronger, or more confident than you are right now. Make it as vivid as you can. Base it on a superhero, an athlete, or an actor if you wish.

2. Do your best to feel the change, and keep it up for at least one minute.

3. Next time you are with people, recall the fantasy and the feeling briefly and notice if anyone else notices anything different about you.

4. Repeat this exercise daily, or several times a day, for a week, and pay attention to how often your imagination pulls you into a different state.

SELF-ESTEEM

Self esteem is a product of perception, recall, and imagination, because it depends entirely on how you perceive yourself, what you recall about yourself, and what you imagine about yourself. It is also the mental framework on which all other personal qualities are built.

Confidence, for instance, is based on authority, but authority is based on the esteem in which someone or something is held. Without that esteem, no authority is granted. If you want to develop your own inner authority, you have to increase your self-confidence; and in order to increase your self-confidence, you have to increase your self-esteem, which is the imagined value that you give to yourself.

Another good reason for increasing your self-esteem is that doing so has a direct effect on how others value you, too. Self-esteem is almost as vital to effective relationships as the air we breathe, the water we drink, and the food we eat, because it is our own measure of our own value as a human being. If we think of ourselves as worthless, then we open our lives to the worst kinds of exploitation. And if we do not respect ourselves, very few others will respect us, either.

On the other hand, many cultures, including our modern one, have strong inhibitions about thinking well of oneself. The English expressions accusing someone of having a "swelled head," or of being "too big for his britches" or "snobbish," or of thinking that she is "better than we are" are routinely applied to people who express some degree of self-appreciation, and in some cultures it is considered the height of bad manners to have a good self-concept. This becomes more curious and confusing when you realize that the most successful people in any society obviously have very high self-esteem and that most self-help programs strongly promote it. Why, then, does this subject inspire such opposing points of view?

Cultural Conflicts

At one time or another, most cultures of the world have made strong class or caste distinctions that exalt a small minority over a much larger majority. Not only are the minority considered intrinsically better in most cases, the majority are usually considered intrinsically bad. Some people in the Hawaiian aristocracy often even referred to the commoners as dirt, or excrement.

Very typical of this pattern was the Natchez society of the lower Mississippi Valley in the central United States. Considered a last remnant of the ancient mound-building culture of North America, the society was described by seventeenth-century French explorers. At the top of the social pyramid was a ruler with absolute power, the Great Sun. Just below him were his relatives, the Lesser Suns. Then came a class of nobles; a class of lesser nobles, or honored ones; and, finally, the mass of commoners who were contemptuously called "Stinkards." This pattern has a familiar ring to it all over the world.

At some point in a society's development, divisions of labor make sense, including the mental/emotional labor of leadership and administration. But that kind of labor is so important, and the ones who are really good at it are so few, that social value often gets mixed up with individual value, so that the leaders also become thought of as better people. A real problem arises when the nonleaders as a group become thought of as lesser people, and talented individuals born into that group find it difficult, dangerous, and perhaps impossible to move out of the group and use their abilities.

What does this occurrence have to do with self-esteem today? The cultural legacy of class distinctions that most of us have received from our ancestors still lingers in overt and subtle ways. Even "enlightened" modern Western societies show a strong, ongoing tendency to endow the entitled, the wealthy, the educated, and—to some degree—the exceptionally talented with superior qualities as individuals, regardless of their behavior, and to endow the less privileged as inferior individuals, again regardless of their behavior.

Like it or not, we still find these attitudes common regarding contrasting groups of the rich and famous versus the poor and unknown; white collar versus blue collar workers; the college-educated versus those who are not; and, of course, racial groups. Also, the remembered dangers of competing against your "betters" still exist. I can remember my Italian mother saying to me once long ago when I was planning my way to fame and fortune, "Be careful that you don't make the gods jealous." The "gods" don't always refer to heavenly beings: they can also be a symbol of those with political and economic power. Because high self-esteem is associated with standing out from the crowd, and standing out carries with it cultural memories of danger from jealous rulers, children today are often given subtle but pervasive hints to blend in, to not rock the boat, to refrain from doing anything that would bring too much attention to themselves. Of course, there are exceptional people who do outstanding things without regard to the opinion of others, but what makes them so fascinating as items for gossip and storytelling is that they are exceptional.

However, high self-esteem is not the problem, and it wouldn't be so important were excessively *low* self-esteem not so prevalent. For it is low self-esteem—a sense of unworthiness and disrespect for oneself—that reduces our ability to stand up for our rights when we are being exploited, cheated, or abused; to say "NO" when it is in our best interests to do so; and to pursue the development of good relationships.

Religious Inhibitions

In the interest of helping people become more flexible and open to spiritual influence, major Western and Eastern religions have tended to emphasize humility as a virtue and pride as a sin. Individual leaders may have misused such teachings for their own ends from time to time. Nevertheless, realizing that you yourself may not have all the answers for solving life's problems and that you are not inherently better than everyone else can be healthy. Unfortunately, though, these essentially good ideas frequently become distorted in practice.

Humility is false, for instance, when you suppress your natural talents and abilities for the sake of getting approval. In doing so you will be living a lie that will take its physical, emotional, and mental toll on you. That kind of humility is neither spiritual nor beneficial to you or to your community.

By the same token, pride is not sinful when it is based on an honest recognition of who you are and what you can do. But some people believe so strongly that any form of self-recognition is bad that they go out of their way to squelch all appreciation of anyone's goodness, especially their own and that of their family. In what is perhaps a well-intentioned effort, many not only suppress the recognition of goodness and improvement, they also negate it most thoroughly with that all-time destroyer of self esteem: the terrible social weapon of criticism.

Nevertheless, if you think about it you will understand that true pride and true humility are one and the same. Each one involves an honest appraisal of your state as a human being and of your place in the world. If you think of that state and place as good, you have a healthy self-esteem. If you consider them bad but think you can learn how to change them, then you can develop a healthy self-esteem. But if you think that your state of being and your place in the world are bad and you don't deserve any better, your low self-esteem will always get in the way of your happiness and success.

More on Self-Criticism

When I was in high school, I liked my science teacher and loved science, but I was bored by the way it was taught and slacked off on my homework. The teacher, apparently trying out some student psychology he had learned, began criticizing me in class for all sorts of things in the vain hope of spurring me on to greater effort. I reacted by moving away from the criticism instead and took to spending the science hour in the local pool hall. I got pretty good at pool, but I graduated high school with a D– average, number sixty-four in a class of sixty-five.

I can't blame my science teacher for that poor grade, nor can I blame any of the other teachers who used criticism as a teaching method. They were doing what they'd been taught to do, and my reactions were my own. I rebelled and withdrew because my own self-criticism was so heavy I couldn't handle any more.

Parents are the next easy target for blame. Maybe my self-criticism came from their criticism of me. To be sure, my father was pretty critical, in my opinion, although far less critical than his father had been to him. My mother's criticism was more subtle: she was always telling me how much potential I had, which I interpreted to mean that I wasn't okay the way I was.

Still, my parents were just trying to help me become a better person and do better in school. I was the one who took their criticism so negatively. So, was my response my fault? No, I wasn't to blame, either, because I didn't know how to react differently. I had no model or training for dealing with criticism in a more positive way.

Then was it society's fault? No, because "society" does not really exist as an independent being with the power of self-aware action. It is only an artificial idea that we use to talk about a bunch of people who share certain kinds of behavior and boundaries. Society can't be at fault for anything.

No, my reactions at that time weren't anyone's fault. The whole process of finding fault is based on the practice of looking for what is wrong so that we can fix it. That's not a bad practice for working on machines, but it is extremely inefficient when working with people. The most efficient way to change human behavior, including your own, is to reinforce what's right, not try to fix what's wrong. Criticism, however well meant, has the opposite effect to the one intended because it is based on fear, rather than on love. The desire for approval is one of the strongest of all human motivations. The loss of approval is one of our greatest fears. This is why criticism has such power; it is an expression of disapproval. It is bad enough when someone you care for or need disapproves of you in some way, but it is literally disabling when you disapprove of yourself. You can always move away from someone else's influence, or change your behavior to please them (well, maybe not always). But if you disapprove of yourself you are stuck, because you can't get away and even changing your behavior may not work. I recall the story of a man who smoked for thirty years and finally gave it up because his church said it was sinful, but he felt continually guilty and unhappy because he could not forgive himself for having done something so bad for so long.

The worst criticism of all is self-criticism, especially if it is based on the idea that you are no good no matter what. If this is your problem, only you can make the decision to think differently about yourself. And as much as you may want to help someone else who is highly self-critical, only they can make the same decision. One of the most frustrating things you can do is try to convince someone that they are good when they don't think so. It's like trying to give someone a piece of cake through a screen. It can be seen as good, smelled as good, but it just doesn't reach them. They've got to make their own cake and eat it before the screen can come down and they can share cake with you.

On the other hand, self-criticism does have some positive benefits, surprisingly. In some cases it can make you so angry with yourself that you begin to make changes. And it's an effective technique for avoiding risk. If you criticize yourself just the right amount, in just the right way, you can convince yourself that you don't have the talent, skill, nerve, or right to try something new (and possibly make a fool of yourself). So self-criticism can be used to avoid a potential loss of approval, self- or otherwise.

But of course I'm speaking tongue in cheek here; as a life principle, self-criticism would be stultifying. Whatever benefits it might occasionally provide cannot make up for the havoc self-criticism wreaks on your life when it becomes a habit. We can all live with occasional self-criticism, even if we would be better off without it. But habitual self-criticism is devastating. It makes it practically impossible ever to feel good about anything you do, since you will automatically put yourself down as soon as good feelings begin. Suppose you were a person with an HSC (Habitual Self-Criticism) syndrome. If you won an Oscar for acting—one of the highest professional awards—you might feel an initial flush of pleasure at the announcement, but then you would find fault with the way you were dressed, the way you walked up to the podium, the way you said thank you, the way you returned, and no doubt with the performance that had won you the award as well. In a short time the thrill of recognition will have turned to ashes. People who are habitual self-criticizers rarely enjoy anything for long.

Self-criticism also interferes with developing talents and skills. A common assumption is that it helps improve behavior and increase achievement, but the contrary is true if the self-criticism becomes habitual. We learn better and faster by reward rather than by punishment. As I've mentioned, babies learn to walk and speak by focusing on what they do right and repeating it, not by remembering what they do wrong and avoiding it. The greater our reward for a correct action, the more eagerly we repeat the action and thereby improve our skill. But the greater the punishment for any action—and all criticism is felt as punishment—the more we avoid that action as much as we can.

If the positive benefit of an action is great enough, we will persist in it in spite of criticism—as a young man might persist in serving tables because the tips are so good, even though his father criticizes him for having such a menial job. At the same time, though, the criticism creates a subconscious resistance to the action—as, in our example, the young man may resent serving tables, even while he continues to do so. Such resistance to what we are in fact nevertheless *doing* makes the whole process of improvement much harder. And if the criticism is constant and comes from the self instead of from others, everything we do becomes much more difficult.

Self-criticism diminishes the quality of our relationships. The more critical you are of yourself, the more critical you will tend to be with others and the more critical they will tend to be of you. The habit of inner-directed criticism easily extends outward. People with good self-esteem do not enjoy being around highly self-critical people, not only because it is unpleasant in itself, but because they can sense themselves being criticized, consciously or subconsciously, as well. Criticism is not limited to verbal disapproval, you see. It can also be perceived in all your facial expressions and body movements. So, if you are habitually self-critical, the usual result is that you are left with other highly self-critical people, and you all just reinforce one another's behavior.

The Pain of Perfection

To be perfect seems like such a good ideal. To be faultless, without flaw, untarnished and pure—how wonderful!

The real problems that arise from pursuing that ideal do not come from the ideal itself but from the interpretation of what perfection means. To be faultless implies some standard to go by. But where does that standard come from? The Ten Commandments? The Eight-fold Path of Buddha? The Laws of the Koran? Family values? Society's laws? A teacher's rules? Your own decisions about right and wrong? Are you perfect if you follow one set of guidelines and not another? For instance, are you perfect if you follow your father's rules of behavior and not your mother's. Or vice versa? And if you fail to meet the standard you accept, what does that mean? Can you redeem yourself by "correcting" your behavior, or are you forever condemned because you slipped however many times? I'm not providing answers here; I'm raising questions to think about. You have a right to follow any standard you choose and to determine whether not meeting it means you are faulty (as opposed to meaning you simply didn't conform to a standard set by you or someone else). If your standards aren't clear and consistent, then your feelings, attitudes, and behavior toward yourself won't be clear or consistent, either.

What is a flaw? Some people believe that all humans are flawed. If so, then as long as you are human you are going to be imperfect, and it makes more sense to accept that than to fight it and feel bad about it for the rest of your life. Some people believe that so-called character or physical "defects" are signs of flaws. This, however, is a matter of standards again, because what is a defect to one person may be a positive attribute to another. In the laboratory, for instance, it is possible to make sapphires that are totally free from physical defects and consistent in color and quality. But the most valuable sapphires are ones that are dug out of the earth and polished and that have certain visible flaws. Their value comes from their imperfection. In a sense, then, the most perfect sapphire has to be imperfect.

Abraham Lincoln was full of defects, according to detractors during his terms in office. He was called, among other things, "a wet rag," "a weakling," and "the root of evil."

Even his Gettysburg Address was described by the *Chicago Times* as "silly, flat, and dishwatery." Physically, he was perceived by some as awkward, ungainly, and ugly. But his physical presence was still impressive, and it was his character that led our nation into a new era. Was he perfect? It all depends on what you consider as flaws.

Along the same lines, it is interesting to note that a garden with weeds is considered flawed, yet a weed is just a plant growing where we don't think it should. A flowering plant called *lantana* is carefully cultivated in California as an ornamental, but in Hawaii it is a weed wildly overtaking native plants. Qualities that define you as flawed in one part of the world or in one period of your life may define you as perfect in another. Intellectuals may be unfit for the gym but successful in the laboratory; athletes may stumble in the library but excel in the arena. So, again, what is a flaw?

The word *untarnished* generally means *polished* in the sense that the true nature of a thing shines clearly, uncontaminated by contact with something that might lower its value. *Untarnished* makes us think of shiny metal, like gold, silver, and brass, or of people with unsullied reputations who have never done what some would call wrong.

Again, it sure sounds good. Realistically, though, polished metals can be useful as well as beautiful, but so can tarnished ones. The green patina of bronze, for instance, is a desirable condition that enhances its beauty. And anodized aluminum is purposely tarnished to protect and beautify it. With people, the "tarnish" gives them experience that can be extremely valuable in teaching or helping others.

Think of such groups as Alcoholics Anonymous and the prisoners who teach young people how not to go to prison. Sometimes the person with the perfectly untarnished reputation is the most imperfect one for the job.

How about being pure? Now there's a loaded concept! Take the idea of racial purity, for example. There isn't any such animal. Everyone has a mixed heritage, and it doesn't take much research to find it out. Some people decide on their own that certain racial mixtures aren't good, but that's just a made-up rule for which there is no justification in nature. It used to be common, and it is still fairly current, to think of purity in terms of sexual conduct. Sexual fantasies are called "impure thoughts," and sexual behaviors that don't follow some group's arbitrary rules are called "impure acts." People who have engaged in such thoughts or acts are said to have polluted themselves and must be cleansed. I don't have any interest in what your particular rules for sexual conduct are, but I am interested in clear thinking and speaking. If you want to define certain behavior as pure and other behavior as impure, and decide that certain acts are polluting and other acts are cleansing, then go ahead and enjoy (or dread) the consequences. Just remember that the decisions are yours and no one else's. Even if you think the rules come from a perfect source, it is your decision to follow them or not.

The whole idea of purity as an ideal comes from the assumption that the more sameness there is the better. Yet, we don't find this at all in the world around us. Absolutely pure water—distilled water—is man made, and it is dead water. To nourish us it needs minerals, flora and fauna,

H_2O_2, and electrical charges. Then it is living water. The beauty of an amethyst comes from iron impurities that turn the quartz purple. All of our basic foods, even the organically-grown and pesticide-free ones, are hybrids. All work and no play make Jack a dull boy, and variety is the spice of life.

The ideal of perfection may also give rise to an attempt to reach an unchanging, "perfect" state of mind, body, or circumstance. In this case, once a state is reached that is defined as perfect, then any change in that state must represent imperfection. If a perfect day is thought of as a bright sun shining in a clear blue sky, then a single cloud would "mar" that perfection, even though it would be a natural event. If a perfect body is supposed to look like the model in the magazine and yours doesn't, then yours is obviously imperfect. If a perfect mind is supposed to think only good thoughts and you happen to be upset for a moment because your soul mate didn't take out the garbage, then your mind is imperfect.

Ideals are good to have, but when anything less than the ideal is called "bad," trouble is on the way. More specifically, if you think of yourself as bad whenever you are imperfect (according to your own ideals), then you are in for a lot of unhappiness and failure, because the idea of perfection as an unchanging state holds a deadly trap. The trap is hidden in the assumption that any state of mind, body, or circumstance can be unchanging. If you actually allow yourself to observe and study yourself and the world around you, it will soon be clear that nothing ever remains the same—not stars, mountains, seasons, events, people, and certainly not you. Now, you can fault yourself for every time your internal or external behavior doesn't match your ideal and thereby frequently cause yourself to suffer from low self-esteem, or you can applaud the changes you like, tolerate the ones you don't, and treat perfection as a journey rather than as a place to be.

Seven Techniques for Self-Esteem

It is one thing to understand low self-esteem and why you might have it and quite another to do something about it. Here are some ways and means that work. These techniques can be done as a seven-minute exercise, spending one minute on each one in turn, or individually whenever you think they are appropriate:

I Am What I Am. This was a favorite saying of the cartoon character Popeye. He would also, from time to time, let everyone within hearing distance know in no uncertain terms that he was a "sailor man." He clearly defined himself, particularly after every success, to reinforce his sense of self-esteem, and you can do the same. The world is what you think it is, and you are what you think you are. To raise your self-esteem and increase your effectiveness, define yourself—honestly—in the most positive way you can. You can do this by saying to yourself, aloud or silently, "I am . . . , " and add any positive quality, attribute, talent, or skill that you can remember. Of course, if you are like many other people, it could be easier at first to come up with negative definitions like, "I am lazy," or, "I am not very good at cleaning house," but do your best to ignore such negatives during this exercise. They may exist, but they're not important right now, and you can do something about them later if you want to. For the moment, concentrate on positive things. Here are some examples just to get you started. Yours may be completely different:

- "I am alive."

- "I am a mother/father" (you can add "good" if you believe it).

- "I am a loyal friend."

- "I am a good worker."

- "I am healthy."

- "I am a . . ." (add your profession, like secretary or sailor man).

Keep repeating your self-definitions for at least one minute. If you can only think of a few at first, just keep repeating them for the whole minute. It may be helpful to write them down, but change or add to the list whenever you want.

Remember When. One of the things that keeps low self-esteem alive is the habit of frequently recalling your mistakes. In this exercise, the purpose is to counteract that effect by purposely recalling situations in which you did something right. Notice that I said, "right," not "perfect." It is always possible for anything to have been done better than it was. The point here is not to review what you could have improved on but to honor yourself for whatever you did that worked, even a little bit. Here are some examples taken from my life:

- The time I first jumped out of a tree.
- The time I got my driver's license.
- The time I got an "A" grade on my term paper.
- The time I won at poker.
- The time I didn't lose my temper when my son rolled my Mustang.

These things don't have to be big triumphs. Even recalling very small successes will help you feel better about yourself. During the minute or more you dwell on these memories, let yourself remember how good you felt at the time, too.

Wannabee. A "wannabee" is a person who "wants to be," that is, who wants to look and/or act like someone else who is admired. There are Elvis wannabees, Marilyn Monroe wannabees, Arnold Schwarzenegger wannabees, Madonna wannabees, and as many others as there are people who symbolize success.

Often wannabees are put down, as if there is something wrong with wanting to be like someone else who already has something you want. You may have been criticized at some point in your life for dressing or acting like someone else and told to "be yourself" instead. What the critic usually means is "don't be anything except what I want you to be." To "be yourself" doesn't have any meaning if you aren't clear about who you are, and "being yourself" can be the worst thing to do if your behavior and habits are mostly negative. Some people, when faced with this problem, go off somewhere to "find themselves," but the main benefit of that is to get away from the critic. You aren't elsewhere. You are right where you are.

Most of what you are, however, is an accumulation of learned attitudes, habits, and behaviors. That's right, "you" are mostly what you have learned to be, and you learned it from someone else. You have your own uniqueness, naturally, but your unique self is like the material on which a portrait is painted. The artist represents the people you learn from; the paint is experience, and the material is you. The same artist using the same paint will produce different effects on canvas, rice paper, cardboard, or silk. All of us learn from the people around us, even when we aren't aware of it, and even when what we learn isn't what we want.

I recall vividly an occasion about twenty years ago when I was very angry at one of my sons, and I had the strangest sensation for a moment that I was my father. It shook me up so much I went off by myself for a while to analyze it. I finally realized that, in that moment, I had been matching almost exactly an anger pattern of my father's that I had incorporated subconsciously. Fortunately for my son, I immediately began practicing a more effective response.

Since we learn attitudes and behaviors from other people anyway, we might as well make a conscious choice of what we want to learn and from whom so that we can raise our self-esteem. That's what the technique of Wannabee is all about. It is not to try to become another person because we don't like ourselves; it is to learn the best of what we can from another person so we can like ourselves even more. The way to practice the Wannabee technique is to think of people who have qualities you would like to have, to decide to develop those qualities in yourself, and then to practice those qualities in your thinking, feeling, and actions by using the other person as your "teacher." You can pick different qualities from different people, and these people might be living or nonliving, real or fiction, famous or local. You could choose the dedication of Mother Theresa, the enthusiasm of your best friend, the poise of Princess Leia (from Star Wars), and the persistence of Mahatma Gandhi. Or anything else you want. The thing to keep in mind is to practice these things to make them your own.

Posturetalk. The way you hold your body not only tells other people a lot about how you think of yourself, it actually affects how you think about yourself. Try this experiment:

1. While sitting in a chair, let your head fall forward.

2. Cross your arms, and then bring one hand up and slightly pull your lower lip out with your thumb and forefinger.

3. After fifteen seconds, take your hand away and uncross your arms. Lift your head and look forward, and place

145

your hands flat on top of your thighs. Hold this position for fifteen seconds.

How did you feel in each position, and what did you think of? How did your feelings and thoughts differ, depending on your position? If you were like most people, you would have felt a bit depressed or uncertain in the first position and a bit more hopeful or certain in the second. Even if you had other reactions to these postural patterns, it is easy to discover the relationship between posture, feelings, and thoughts.

The Posturetalk technique is a way of getting your body to "speak" to your mind and emotions to help them create better self-esteem. To try it, you explore different ways of sitting, standing, walking, moving, and positioning your arms and hands until you find several postures that help you think and feel better. Then you practice those postures until you can do them well whenever you want to. As an alternative, you can remember times when you were at your best and reproduce the postures you held then. I do this sometimes by remembering my best days as a Marine Corps sergeant. An alternative is to practice the postures used by other people who seem to have good self-esteem.

Saturation Praise. The best antidote to self-criticism is self-praise. Wait! Before you back off, I mean deserved praise. To put it another way, you can counteract the esteem-lowering effects of criticism with compliments based on real experience. Such compliments reinforce your self-respect by reminding you that you're not all bad, even if you're not as good as you'd like to be. To be effective as esteem builders and criticism healers, though, the compliments have to be true. They do not, however, have to be world shaking. Acknowledging anything in the least bit worthwhile is useful.

To practice the technique of Saturation Praise, spend a full minute or more giving yourself as many compliments as you can think of without allowing any pause for rebuttal. If you can't think of enough to fill a minute at first, then just keep repeating what you have. Here are examples to get you started:

- I have a nice smile.

- My skin is clear.

- My handwriting is legible.

- I make good brownies.

- My friends can always count on me.

- I never hit little old ladies (unless they hit me first).

Or say whatever suits your life and behavior. When you compliment yourself as directed for a full minute, you will usually feel a lot better. It is important to realize that even a justified criticism does not negate the reality and value of a justified compliment.

Giving Up Guilt. The way to give up guilt is to change your mind about what you did or didn't do. I don't mean to pretend it didn't happen; I mean to change your mind about what it means. This is called self-forgiveness.

Other people can forgive you all they want, but it is what you think about yourself that really matters, and if you don't forgive yourself as a result of their forgiveness, then what they think doesn't matter. Even God can forgive you, but if you don't forgive yourself you will still feel guilty. So what's a person to do? Use the "Giving Up Guilt" technique. This technique is very simple and effective if you do it on a regular basis.

1. Imagine a black file cabinet, two-drawer or four-drawer—it's up to you. Inside this cabinet, representing one area of your memory, are filed away all the things you feel guilty about.

2. Consciously think of an incident, and pull out a file to symbolize it. The file might contain sounds of things said or unsaid, or pictures of things done or undone.

3. Listen and look, and then decide if you can do anything about the incident now. If you *can* do something, decide to do it, put a little red "active" sticker on the file, and put it back in the cabinet.

4. If there is nothing you can do about it now, you may as well forgive yourself (remembering that forgiveness is not approval), so imagine you have a large rubber stamp and stamp "FORGIVEN" on the file. Then put it in a different file cabinet—this time a white one—representing another area of your memory. You can pull the incident out again and feel guilty about it whenever you want, but that's just self-indulgence.

5. Do this exercise with as much detail as you can imagine, and you will truly feel differently about the incident and about yourself. The more often you do it, the better you will feel. If there is a truly major event you feel guilty about, break it up into smaller segments and work on one piece at a time as you feel ready. You can change the colors of the file cabinets, too, if you wish.

Do-Gooder. Self-esteem comes from how we think about ourselves, and how we think about ourselves comes at least partly from a self-assessment of our own actions and non-actions. The previous technique dealt with the past; this one deals with the future.

"Do-Gooder" is just a name for the esteem-building practice of doing something good for someone else, preferably without caring about the credit. You do it because it's good, and you're good because you do it. It doesn't matter if anyone else knows about it. A hard but effective way to practice this is to do small favors for relatives and friends without them asking and perhaps without them being aware of what you've done. Here are some ideas:

- Making beds for someone else.

- Doing dishes without waiting to be asked.

- Washing cars or windows for someone.

- Picking up litter in public places.

- Filling the gas tank when you borrow a car.

- Doing someone else's chores.
- Sharing your favorite treats.

The hard part of this practice is doing such favors for people you know without being openly appreciated. If you find it too hard—that is, if it's too painful for you not to get credit—then it would be better not do it in the first place.

An easier form of "Do-Gooder" that will still work is helping others who are really in need. Here are just a few ideas. If you pay attention, there will undoubtedly be many more opportunities in your community:

- Volunteering for a nonprofit agency
- Supporting ecology groups
- Donating to animal shelters or charities that help people

Self-esteem affects every part of your life. If it is low, your life suffers; if it is good, life is more enjoyable and your relationships are more effective. If you dare to make it high, your performance and your happiness soar out of sight.

Chapter 6

Your Relationship with Your Spirit

This chapter is probably not at all what you thought it was going to be. That's because, in English, the word *spirit* has so many different meanings. The word's most fundamental meaning is "essence." That's all well and good, but there are many ways to think of the essence of something. For some people, *spirit* refers to the essence of alcoholic beverages, produced by a process of distillation, such as brandy, vodka, and gin. However, this chapter is not about alcohol.

For other people, *spirit* refers to nonphysical entities that inhabit material things, like nature spirits; or to entities that used be physical, like the spirits or the dead; or to things that represent the essence of something abstract, like the spirit of a civilization; or to angels and immortal beings vast in scope and beyond our understanding. I'm not talking about any of them here, either.

For still other people, the essence of a human being is a mysterious something called the "soul." This chapter is not about your soul in the way that most people think about it.

What I *am* going to talk about, and provide demonstrations and techniques for, relates to your spirit in terms of energy and how that concerns your relationships in general.

YOUR PHYSICAL ENERGY

I have already talked a little about physical energy when I described how your body transforms sensory information from the world around you into electrical impulses that travel along your nervous system. Now I will go more in depth with this subject.

Without sufficient physical energy, you can't kiss a lover, hug a friend, or run from an enemy. Most people don't give much thought to their physical energy, taking for granted that they either have it or they don't. In fact, an amazing number of people think that energy is a kind of physical substance that can be poured into or drained out of them. Even worse, some people honestly believe that other people can suck out their energy, leaving them depleted and sick. To banish such fears and enable you to have as much energy as you want to for your relationships, I'm going to explain how your physical energy system really works.

Cell Energy

Operating muscles, extracting wastes, making new cells, healing wounds, and using your brain are constant, everyday activities that require energy. It's fairly obvious that the food we eat, the water we drink, and the air we breathe all affect the amount of energy we have. They do, of course, but only indirectly.

Our most direct source of energy comes from the molecules of a chemical compound called adenosine triphosphate (ATP), which is created inside our cells. When your body needs energy to do something, the ATP molecules are broken apart. This process releases energy in the form of electron waves that is then available for the body's various activities.

However, to make the ATP molecules in itself takes a lot of energy, so where does *that* energy come from? Here's where water, air, and food come in.

The water you drink provides the environment, and some of the nutrients, in which the chemical and energetic activity of the body can take place. Water itself is a highly energetic substance, constantly breaking itself down and reforming, so it is not impossible that it is also a source of energy for the body, but no well-known studies yet exist along those lines.

Food is the major fuel source for the body, without a doubt. Whether you dine out on pork roast, potatoes, and cabbage with chocolate fudge and ice cream, or whether your dinner consists of a green salad topped with oil and vinegar and lean chicken with an apple for dessert, your body breaks it all down into sugars and fats and the high-energy-potential molecules derived from them. Sugar molecules have a lot of energy, but fat molecules have twice as much. Muscles prefer the fat energy, and the brain and nerve cells can use only the sugar energy. Both the sugar and fat molecules are broken apart inside the cells to release energy for the creation of ATP.

Oxygen from the air plays a vital role in this energy release. Some cells can make ATP without it, but the presence of oxygen in the cells can increase production by eighteen times.

All of this energetic activity produces three side effects: waste products, primarily carbon dioxide and water, most of which is expelled when you exhale; excess fat, most of which is stored where you don't want it; and another form of energy called *heat*.

Heat Energy

Healthy human beings maintain an almost constant body temperature of 37 degrees Celsius, or 98.6 degrees Fahrenheit, although the highest body temperature ever recorded in a healthy person was that of a marathon runner just after a race. His temperature at that moment was 41 degrees Celsius, or 105.8 Fahrenheit—high enough for hospitalization in normal circumstances. Ordinarily, our bodies are very sensitive to internal and external temperature changes, and our perception is sensitive enough to tell us when a lover is in the right mood or a child needs care and attention.

Most people take body heat for granted, unless the temperature goes too far one way or the other, but most of that heat is a by-product of all the molecular activity going on in the cells. Some of our body heat also comes from our surroundings, when the environmental temperature is higher than our body surface temperature, even by just a little.

To maintain its healthy state, the body has to give off excess heat into the environment. It does so mainly by radiation and evaporation (perspiration), although exhaling also plays a role. Certain kinds of mental activity, like meditation or concentration, can stimulate the production of excess heat that the body has to get rid of. When I held meetings at the Aloha International Museum on Kauai in the summer, we used an air conditioner, but the heat radiation of a group of twenty or more people could make the room uncomfortably hot in spite of the air conditioner. The same kinds of mental activity, with a different focus, may actually diminish the production of personal heat.

Our heat energy plays an important role in our relations with other people, because we tend to equate temperature differences with emotional differences. A person with a comfortably warm envelope of air around his or her body is generally considered emotionally warm and pleasant to be with. If the envelope is too warm, however, we feel uncomfortable around that person; the tendency is to interpret excessive warmth as suppressed anger, which it sometimes is. If we perceive that the person's air envelope is comfortably cool, on the other hand, we tend to interpret the coolness as signifying that the person is more intellectual than emotional, or perhaps simply very calm. And if the personal envelope is uncomfortably cool, the interpretation may be that he or she is emotionally aloof or distant. In English, we might call such a person a "cold fish." Sometimes these interpretations are invalid, because there may be purely physiological or mental reasons for the temperature differences. Sometimes, however, emotions really may be involved, and we'll cover that later.

Muscular Energy

Although all muscular activity involves cell energy and heat energy, here I'm going to talk about the use of muscles for movement, posture, and resistance.

It takes energy to move our bodies around; to touch, pick up, or move things; to push; to pull; to react to people, events, and circumstances; to stand; to sit; and even to lie down. It also takes energy not to move, not to feel, and not to react. All of this involves muscular energy.

We use muscular energy to caress or hit someone and also *not* to caress or hit someone. We use muscular energy to express how we feel and to *suppress* how we feel. The state of our muscles has a direct effect on the state of our relationships.

As stated above, people can be very sensitive to the degree of heat your body generates. The same is true for your degree of muscular tension, because this tension affects your movements, your postures, your skin color, and your heat radiation, all of which other people use—consciously or subconsciously—to interpret your state of mind, your feelings, and your intentions.

Basically, muscles relax and contract in response to physical or mental activity and conditions. Dehydration can cause extended contraction (or tension), and rehydration can produce relaxation. Worry can cause contraction, and confidence can cause relaxation.

Generally speaking, encountering someone or something we like tends to induce acceptance and relaxation, while encountering someone or something we *don't* like tends to induce resistance and tension. Interestingly, recalling or anticipating what we like or don't like will have the same effect.

Too much relaxation can be as bad for a relationship as too much tension. It's as hard to have a good time with a limp dishrag as it is with an iron pole. However, since too much tension is much more common, it's good to have a simple way to relax excess tension when you want to.

Here's a simple exercise that is another form of *piko-piko* useful for relaxing and calming down:

1. Sit, stand, or lie down—your choice.

2. Place one or both hands over your navel.

3. As you inhale and exhale, keep your attention on the sensation of your hand(s) against your skin. If you absolutely must do something more with your mind, just think the word *relax* over and over.

4. Continue for at least one or two minutes, the longer the better.

Emotional Energy

Although there is general agreement that people experience emotions, there is no general agreement in the world on what emotions are. Therefore, some of the things I have to say about emotions may not be agreeable to everyone. Nevertheless, I will say them anyway, because these ideas have helped thousands of people to deal with emotions more effectively.

First, we must discard the misguided, ineffective idea that emotions are a material substance such as water, or air, or soil. Even as a metaphor, that doesn't work very well for dealing with them. We don't walk around with our bodies full of emotions, we can't get rid of emotions like we get rid of toxins, and we don't "pick up" emotions from other people like we pick up germs.

Emotions are waves of energy that carry information, similar to the way that microwave-energy waves carry information through the air, or electrical-energy waves carry information through our nervous system. And like sound waves that travel through the air, emotional waves do not exist until something starts them waving. There is no sound until something vibrates strongly enough to create sound waves. There is no emotion until something vibrates strongly enough to create an emotional wave.

I know, I know, this probably goes against everything you've been taught about emotions. Just bear with me and keep an open mind.

You experience emotions when something vibrates. So, what vibrates? The answer is: your muscles. Emotions are energetic reactions to memories or expectations. When an event stimulates a remembrance (without conscious awareness) or a recall (with conscious awareness), and when that switches on important rules about good or bad, pleasure or pain, your muscles react in a way that sends waves of emotional energy through your body and into the world around you. For instance, your body might react emotionally to a smell, a shape, or a particular pattern or intensity of light without your mind knowing why.

And, of course, your mind can react emotionally to any number of things.

An Emotional Experience. The two most important things that determine the nature of an emotional reaction are the rules you have about a memory or expectation and the degree of overall muscle tension currently in your body. Of these two, muscle tension takes precedence.

1. In any comfortable body position, relax all your muscles as completely as you can.

2. While keeping your muscles relaxed, get very angry about something you recall or imagine.

3. If your muscles truly are relaxed, you will find that you simply cannot experience anger.

4. Try the same experiment with fear and you will get the same result.

5. Try the same experiment with joy and you will also get the same result, although you may find the state of relaxation itself to be somewhat pleasurable.

The thing to learn from this exercise is how important your degree of tension—or stress, if you prefer—is to your emotional state. Emotions of any kind require an increase in muscle tension for their existence. Naturally, any muscle activity affects your physical energy, as well. You can, quite literally, become physically exhausted from sustained emotional activity, although your endurance is greater with positive emotions.

Positive and Negative Emotions. Physiologically, both positive and negative emotions only exist in the presence of certain kinds of muscle tension. Negative emotions require a certain level of steadily increasing or sustained muscle tension. If there is too little tension, the negative emotion disappears. If there is too much tension, the negative emotional reaction is suppressed because the muscles cannot move, and the memory that would stimulate the emotional reaction cannot be accessed. Sustained tension at this level unfortunately has many unpleasant side effects on your body, your mind, and your relationships. And please note that it is not the *emotion* that is suppressed; rather, it is the memory or expectation of an event, plus their accompanying rules. Unless they are activated, emotions don't happen.

Positive emotions require steadily increasing or sustained pulsations of muscular tension and relaxation. Without tension, no positive emotion will exist. Without relaxation accompanying the tension, the emotion will cease to be positive. Positive emotions generally have beneficial side effects on your body, your mind, and your relationships.

Emotional Range and Intensity. The English language has dozens of words that describe different positive and negative emotions, but this is misleading. Actually, all human beings only experience two emotions: happiness and unhappiness. All the other words actually only describe variations in associated circumstances and intensity.

Sorrow is an unhappy feeling associated with loss; sadness is an unhappy feeling associated with regret; contentment is a happy feeling associated with a state of wholeness; cheerfulness is a happy feeling associated with free-flowing energy.

An intensification of these experiences, which means an increase in the amplitude of the energy involved, may result in a different name being given to the experience. Thus, intense sorrow may be called *grief*; intense sadness may be called *despair*; intense contentment may be called *fulfillment*; and intense cheerfulness may be called *joy*.

Nevertheless, the basic emotions being expressed all amount to happiness and unhappiness.

The Source of Emotions. I want to make this point very clearly, because it is a radical idea and essential to good relationships: emotions are nothing more, and nothing less, than energetic reactions to your own thoughts.

Let me put it another way: emotions follow thoughts. Are you listening?

One important conclusion from this idea is that other people do not make you happy or unhappy. This concept may go against your entire life pattern for dealing with relationships, but that's the way it is. Some people may give other people the responsibility for their happiness or unhappiness, but that is a misconception. People are happy or unhappy according to how they think about their experiences and for no other reason.

I once attended a conference in Colorado where different teachers, including me, were giving workshops and lectures. One of the teachers was a young Frenchman whose name I do not remember, unfortunately. His topic was "How to Be Happy." I wasn't able to attend his workshop, but I did go to his lecture, and it was an effort to keep from laughing and crying all the way through it.

The problem was not his concept, which was excellent (meaning that I agreed with it wholeheartedly), but that so few people in the audience could understand it. Some of the dialogue during the question and answer period went like this:

Student A:	"But what if my husband left me?"
Teacher:	"Be happy."
Student B:	"But what if I lose my job?"
Teacher:	"Be happy."
Student C:	"But what if I get sick?"
Teacher:	"Be happy."

The teacher was sincere, but the students couldn't get it. His message was simply that happiness is a choice, while the students could not let go of the idea that people and circumstances dictate happiness.

Of course, it's difficult to be happy when a marriage breaks up or a job is lost or someone gets sick. Difficult, yes, but not impossible. It's not impossible, because the feeling comes from you, not from elsewhere. Here's how it works:

A. Someone does something.

B. Your body reminds you of the related rules.

C. You opt to accept the rule or change it.

D. Your body reacts emotionally according to your decision.

People generally have the most trouble with the "C" part, because they've developed a habit of accepting the current rules without question so quickly that they go directly from "A" to "D" without a break and without realizing that a decision was made.

How do I know this is the way it is? Well, it's my theory based on helping hundreds of people to change their emotional reactions in just a few moments by consciously changing their rules.

A Fast Technique for Changing Rules. In my book, *Healing for the Millions,* I describe a very fast way to change emotional reactions. Here is another fast, nonverbal technique called TFR (Think, Feel, Relax):

1. Think of a situation in your life that typically produces an unhappy reaction.

2. Locate the place in your body where you feel this reaction.

3. Concentrate all of your attention on relaxing that part of your body.

4. When that part of your body feels better, think of the situation again and note any change in your reaction.

5. Repeat, if necessary, until you have no more unhappy reaction when you think of the situation.

The only problem with this technique is that some people think it is too simple to work. Well, it does work, but you have to try it.

Mental Energy

Every time you think a thought you cause a ripple in the fabric of the universe. It isn't a big ripple, of course, but it doesn't have to be big in order to produce a big effect. After all, when a giant tree is ready to fall, the gentle touch of a finger will finish the job. Likewise, the right thought at the right time can affect the whole world.

Your thoughts have the greatest influence on your own body. Every single thought you have will produce some degree of reaction in your cells. Some thoughts will only have an insignificant effect on a few cells, and some thoughts will stimulate radical changes in major organs and muscles.

One year I went skiing in the mountains of California when it was bitterly cold. While riding in a long chair lift my gloved hands got so cold I was afraid they would freeze. So I imagined that my hands were close to a warm campfire and mentally repeated the words "my hands are warm" over and over. In about five minutes, my hands were toasty warm inside the gloves. The true significance here is that in order for my hands to become warm in that environment, information had to leap throughout my nervous system; a multitude of muscle cells had to relax and contract and relax to produce extra heat; veins, arteries, and capillaries had to relax; blood flow had to increase; my lymph system had to become more active; and probably even more stuff had to happen. And all I did was to *think* of fire and mentally repeat some words.

In some of my classes, I demonstrate a phenomenon called "telekinesis," the ability to move matter with the mind.

It's very simple. All I do is to ask someone in the audience to hand me a pen. Ta-da! Instant telekinesis. With the power of my mind alone, expressed in words, I have caused a pen to move from ten to fifteen feet away right to my hand. Now, that might sound like a joke, but it isn't. What I did was to use a thought to stimulate an existing behavior pattern—in this case the natural desire on the part of someone to be helpful—in order to move an object without any effort on my part. The implication is that thoughts are most powerful when they work with existing energy patterns rather than against them.

I want to emphasize that it isn't the amount of energy in the thought itself that makes the difference, because thoughts don't put out very much energy. The greatest effect of a thought comes from its ability to stimulate, switch on, or recall an existing behavior pattern that *does* produce or release a lot of energy. This happens most frequently and powerfully when a thought relates directly to one or more rules governing the primary motivations of love, power, or harmony. In particular, when mental energy turns on emotional energy, the effects can be widespread, involving local groups and even nations. I'll have more to say about this in later chapters.

Subtle Energy

This section may require a bit of mind-stretching for some people, because it borders on an area of knowledge usually considered esoteric. So far I have talked about your physical energy, which includes heat and other radiant energy from your body; your emotional energy, which affects your body and your mind; and your mental energy, which affects your emotions and your body. Now it's time to bring up your subtle energy, which involves interactions with your environment that go beyond your physical actions, the sounds you make, and the odors you give off.

This subtle energy is easiest to conceive of as a field through which other waves of energy can flow. A good analogy would be the envelope of air that surrounds the earth. The air itself is a field of energy that is also a medium for sound waves. In a similar way, your subtle energy field is a medium for emotional, mental, and other energy waves.

Some teachings call this subtle energy field the *aura*, and that's as good a name as any, though I prefer the Hawaiian term, *hoaka*. In any case, it is through your aura, or hoaka, that you are able to exchange emotional and psychic information with other people. Intuition, premonitions, hunches, shared emotions, and healing influences all operate through the medium of your subtle energy field.

The energy of your aura can be expanded, contracted, focused, and channeled in a number of different ways for a number of different purposes by using the power of your mind to give it direction.

A Subtle-Energy Experience. This exercise will help to give you a tangible experience of your subtle energy:

1. Hold your hands about six to eight inches (fifteen to twenty centimeters) apart with your palms facing each other.

2. Inhale with your attention on your navel, and exhale with your attention centered in the space between your hands. Do this about four times.

3. Next, push your hands very slightly toward each other with a gentle, bouncing motion. If you are like most people, at this point you will experience a sensation of pressure, as if you were pressing against a soft balloon, and perhaps other sensations as well. If you do have this experience, you are feeling the effects of an intensification of your subtle energy field in the space between your hands.

When your aura is "charged" with mental and/or emotional energy, it can have a strong effect on how other people perceive you. People who seem to have a lot of charisma have a highly charged subtle-energy field. Although some people charge their field naturally without realizing what they are doing, it is also possible to do it consciously and to develop it as a skill.

Charging Your Aura. Here is one way to begin becoming more charismatic:

1. Think of your aura, or at least assume that it exists around you.

2. Use your imagination and/or memory recall to get as excited as you can. Memories of happiness, fun, or laughter work well for this.

3. Interact with people and note how they react to you.

CHAPTER 6

Your Source of Energy

The subject of this section is not God, however you interpret the Divine. Personally, I believe that everything in the universe has one source, but this belief isn't what I'm discussing now. Instead, I want to talk about an aspect of you that extends beyond your body, your mind, and your various forms of energy. It's based on an idea that you are more than any of those things—that there is a part of you that exists beyond time and space and yet within it at the same time. You can think of it as a theory, of course, because whatever we believe about anything is theoretical to someone. My concern is not to get you to believe in what I'm talking about. It's to get you to consider using it for practical purposes. But in order to do that effectively, we have to give it a name. *Spirit* will not work, because that word has too many meanings in English and does not translate well into other languages. *'Aumakua* and *Kane* are Hawaiian words that could be used, but they also have other meanings that might confuse people. I have used Max Long's term *Higher Self* in my writings, but I'm not happy with it because it implies a hierarchical relationship that really isn't part of my tradition. So, I'm going to break new ground and call this aspect your *Greater Self*.

Regardless of other considerations, the primary, practical, and personal usefulness of the Greater Self is as a source of inspiration. Other uses are applicable to your relationships with other people and the world in general, but we'll get to those later.

Inspiration has two important meanings in this context. One is the idea of being inspired with energy, and the other is the idea of being inspired with ideas. Thus, we can speak of a person being inspired to do something without consciously thinking about it, and we can speak of a person being inspired to think of a new way to solve a problem.

Everyone is inspired in some way at some time, and for most people it probably just happens when it happens. Some people recognize that it comes when they need it. Smart people find a way to induce it when they want it. What follows is one simple way to do that.

How to Ask for Inspiration. Be forewarned: this is one of those techniques that work in spite of its absurd simplicity:

1. Find a quiet space and either look at or imagine something beautiful, and experience how that feels.

2. Assume you have a Greater Self and ask it for inspiration—either as energy or guidance or both—for something you need or want. To increase focus, think of your Greater Self as an invisible presence filling you, surrounding you, and extending out beyond you as far as you can imagine.

3. Trust that you will get what you ask for in some way or another. There is no way to tell ahead of time how or when the inspiration will manifest. It may come immediately as a flash of feeling or insight, as words or images now or later, or through someone or something in your environment at a time when you are doing

something else. All you have to do is to trust that the inspiration will come and to pay attention.

A friend of mine who used to own a bookstore told me of a time when she needed inspiration for something important. As she walked down an aisle of her store, a book fell on her head. She was so involved with her thinking that she just reached down, picked up the book, and put it back on a shelf. A few days later the book fell again. This time she looked at it, wondered why it didn't look familiar, and put it back on the shelf. When the book fell a third time, she finally checked her records and found that she had never ordered it. The book was one of mine, *Kahuna Healing,* and it was what brought us together.

Every time I ask a workshop audience if they ever needed inspiration and a book practically jumped out at them in a bookstore, I almost always get a 100 percent response. I get a lot of positive responses when I ask about the mediums of radio, television, and movies, too. Inspiration can also come from children, strangers, or even billboards. I prefer to think that it comes from the Greater Self, but you can credit any source you choose. The most important thing is that it happens.

Part 3

WHY CAN'T WE ALL JUST GET ALONG?

Chapter 7

Healing Family Relationships

Although I began with the importance of healing your relationship with yourself, the way you behave with yourself is usually learned within the context of a family group. That usually means that most of what you know about relationships was learned from your parents. When a mother bird lays eggs, she sits on them until they hatch, and then she feeds the young until they are ready to fly. In some species the male feeds the female until the eggs hatch, and in others the male shares hatching duties and then the feeding duties. After taking good care of their young up to a certain age, Momma and Poppa Bird demonstrate the art of flying and encourage them to take off. If they don't want to take off they are kicked out of the nest. In most mammal groups, the young are protected and fed and trained until they are old enough and smart enough to feed themselves. Then they are pushed away from the mother's teat and either sent off to fend for themselves or given a place in the hierarchy of the group, which affords them protection in return for a contribution of skills and service.

Of all animals on earth, human beings take the longest to mature. They need to be cared for and protected and trained for many years before they are ready to fend for themselves or to help support the group. In most traditional societies, this process can take as long as fourteen years. Oddly, in modern society, it either takes many more years or never seems to end. Not only do many people not want to stop being children, many people don't want to stop being parents, either.

Why many people would not want to stop being children is understandable. They are no different than the young birds who are reluctant to leave a nice, cozy nest where all their needs are taken care of. It's tough for a bird, or a mammal, or a human to get out there and take care of itself and find a mate and raise a family—or even just take care of itself. But humans and other animals are not fully grown until they can do that. Of course, human society provides for a lot of cooperation and help. For all their faults, human beings are the most helpful creatures on earth. The more willing a person is to help him- or herself, the more help he or she will find.

At first glance, it is harder to understand why someone would want to maintain control over one's children long past the time when they ought to be taking care of themselves and helping to support their society. The answer is simple, though: it is fear. That's the only reason people try to control other people. There may be many reasons for the fear, but that doesn't make the desire to control a good thing. Such parental control only serves to stunt the growth of the children, whether the "parent" is a person or a group or a government. If you love someone, don't just set them free. Help them learn how to fly first.

THE PARENTAL DILEMMA

It isn't easy to be a parent. Depending on your parents, of course, it isn't easy to be a child, either. However, the reason it isn't easy to be a child is that it isn't easy to be a parent.

A very, very long time ago, when the majority of human beings were organized into tribes, clans, and/or tightly-knit family groups, parenting was a social skill that one learned along with others close in age and with a lot of support from relatives. Grandparents, younger siblings, uncles, aunts, and cousins all participated in the rearing of children according to the standards of their particular culture. The extended family structure provided a sense of personal security in knowing one's place in the group and the rules of behavior toward other group members. Some moderately extended families today still enjoy this benefit, and the results can be seen in the overall positive behavior of the children. Unfortunately, though, most of our modern, urban world isn't like that anymore. There has been so much social change and disruption worldwide that a typical family group today consists of parents and children and that's it. Any other relatives are typically scattered all over the place.

A major effect of this lack of cohesion is that huge numbers of young adults get married and have children without any idea of how to rear them. I am reminded of an orphaned kitten that my family took care of when we lived on a farm. It grew into a healthy young cat, and on one of its outings it encountered a male cat that had its way with her. We noticed that she was pregnant and didn't think much about it. When she was obviously close to term, we prepared a comfortable box for her to have her kittens in. She gave birth to three tiny kittens without much fuss, but then she just got up and walked away. To our great puzzlement, she wouldn't have anything to do with them and treated them like strangers. We finally realized that she had had no social context—no cat-family experience—to help her understand what the phenomenon of parenthood was all about.

Human parents who lack child-rearing models may act in a similar way, but at least they usually have access to books and support groups if they care enough. However, my point here is the general lack of child-rearing training in the culture. When people have to do something even though they don't know what to do, they do the best they can. And that means they draw from whatever knowledge or experience they can find in order to manage the behavior of these crying, screaming, messy, demanding, rebellious, reckless, and wild things called *children*.

How to Handle Children

As the father of three boys and the grandfather of five girls and three more boys, all I can do is to share some of the things I've learned as they grew up. The most important thing I can say is that children need love more than any-thing else. You can be a pitiful parent in every other way, but if you give them enough love they will turn out fine. Not perfect, by any means, but fine.

For you just to think that you love them is not enough. Children aren't mind readers. They need to feel loved. And when they feel loved they feel more secure, and they have less need to seek love and power in strange ways and in strange places with strange people.

So, how can you make them feel loved? The truth is, you can't. In spite of your best efforts, children are going to feel however they decide to feel. Nevertheless, there are some things you can do that will greatly increase the chances of their feeling more loved than not.

Guidelines

Children need guidelines for how to behave in and cope with the world. They do not need a long list of rules, restrictions, and regulations designed to make the parents feel better. They need the best guidelines you can give them about right and wrong, about what is appropriate and inappropriate, about what works and what doesn't work, about what is legal and illegal. As they grow, they'll hear lots of other ideas from other people, and they'll often be inclined to test and experiment. But the more practical the guidelines you give them, the more likely they are to return to them and pass them on.

Therefore, I recommend explaining the reasons behind your guidelines from the time you first start giving them.

A baby in a crib is not a blank slate. He or she is a human being trying to learn as much and as fast as possible about how to live effectively. Even a baby listens to what you say and will respond in some degree to your explanations of why things are the way they are and why you are asking for the behavior you want.

Respect

Many parents treat their children like slaves or servants, or even necessary inconveniences. It's probably because they themselves were treated that way. This method does not help to produce happy children or effective future parents, however. Also, it does not produce respect for the parents.

True respect has to come from the heart. The appearance of respect in the form of obedience to rules is just play-acting based on fear. The way to gain true respect is to give it freely. If you treat people, including children, with respect, they will tend to respect you. It's as simple as that.

Treating a child with respect means that when you tell a child what to do, you listen to what he or she thinks about it, and then you either change your directive or explain why you can't. This approach doesn't guarantee happiness or compliance, but it does establish a better relationship. Having respect for the child also means paying attention to what the child wants or does and giving importance to his or her concerns. And it means involving the child in major family decisions. It does not mean letting the child run the family; it means acknowledging the child as a participating member of the family.

Social Contact

Human beings bond by doing things together in a way that produces emotional rapport. Otherwise, merely doing things together isn't enough. People who work together on a business or scientific project do not necessarily experience any degree of bonding. On the other hand, people who do something enjoyable or dangerous together *do* tend to bond. In some families, bonding takes place through touching. The Italian side of my family did a great deal of hugging, and hand-shaking, and touching and kissing, in public and in private. That is not to say that they always got along with each other, but a strong sense of family connection always underlay any disagreement—reinforced, of course, by extended family gatherings. It took my father, with his English background, and my wife, with her German/English background, quite a while to get used to so much physical contact.

Other families bond emotionally by participating in group activities, like sports, hiking and camping, or parties. In others, bonding can even come about by sharing more intellectual activities.

The key factor in bonding is the emotional connection. To be effective as a means of bonding, an activity has to stimulate feelings associated with love, in the form either of enjoyment or of mutual support. That is, bonding does not come from the activity itself, but from the emotional experience of the activity. An activity that stimulates bonding during one phase of family interaction will not necessarily have the same effect during another phase.

For instance, just because children enjoyed camping with their parents when they were pre-teens doesn't mean that they will still want to do it when they are older and seeking bonds with their peers. Forcing a child to engage in an activity that he or she no longer enjoys may weaken the bond through resentment, rather than strengthen it. If the parents are flexible enough to change family activities, or even to encourage the children to enjoy positive bonding with other groups, the original family bonds will remain intact because the memories will still be enjoyable.

An Exercise for Parents

When children grow up and become adults, it is important to realize that they are no longer children. Unfortunately, in the eyes of many parents, their children are always children, which can get in the way of good relating. The fact that in English and other languages there is no separate word for *grown-up children* makes it even more difficult. The English word *adolescent* refers to someone who is between puberty and adulthood, neither a child nor an adult. The following exercise is designed to help parents stop thinking of their adult children as the little ones they once were:

1. Imagine that you are in some pleasant location—indoors or outdoors, at home or elsewhere—and that your children are with you as they were before they were adolescents.

2. In this pleasant place in your mind, imagine your children growing into the adults that they are now.

3. Still in your mind, give each of your children a gift to celebrate the fact that they are now adults. This could be a piece of special jewelry, a flower lei, or anything else you choose to represent this special occasion.

4. Finally, give each adult child a wish for happiness and success and send them into the world, away from your location and out of sight. Remember, this is a symbolic departure from the state of childhood; it does not mean that your adult children actually have to go out of your life.

How to Handle Parents

Whether we like it or not, parents play a major role in shaping our lives. First and foremost, they provide the ancestral DNA that forms our bodies and deeply influences our physical, emotional, and mental growth. This is a fundamental factor in our life experience that permeates everything we do. Fortunately, it does not control us, because we are not machines, not just duplicates of our parents. We have spirit and will and the power of choice. We are the builders of our own lives, but we have to use the material our parents have given us to build with.

After birth—and, in this modern age of assisted reproductive technology, sometimes even before birth, we may or may not have any more direct connection with our parents. Some people are raised by their parents, some by relatives, and some are adopted, officially or unofficially. In any case, the people who raise us play a parental role that influences us strongly throughout our lives. Whether we accept their ways or rebel against them, their influence remains strong.

Authority figures such as teachers, leaders, idols, employers, and all others who guide our behavior with or without our consent have a parental influence as well. In my first year at the University of Colorado, when I was married with a child and three years of military service behind me, the university administrative office insisted that I get my mother's signature on a student loan form. I thought the requirement was silly, because at the time I was an adult with a family myself, and I was also helping to support my mother who had very little income. However, the university had a policy for dealing with students called *in loco parentis*, which meant that in the absence of a parent the university itself would act as a parent. And that meant that if Daddy University said I needed Mommy's signature, then I had to get it, regardless of the circumstances.

Parental influence has a much deeper effect than most of us realize. At one time I thought I had rid myself of my own parents' strong influences. I still admired and used my father's teachings, and I still ate many of the foods my mother had fed me, but I didn't think their sway went much beyond that. But then I learned a simple technique for looking at our relationship differently.

A Parental Awareness Technique

You can use this technique as regards your birth parents or any other important parental figure in your life:

1. Think of your most important likes and dislikes, your most important accomplishments, your most important goals, and your most important values of right and wrong, good and bad.

2. Identify the same things for each of your parents, as far as your knowledge allows.

3. Find as many instances as you can of matches and opposites.

This last step was a huge surprise for me, because I had never considered my parents in this way before. Here are a few things that I found in relation to my father:

Regarding opposites, my father never did understand money, and I've gone out of my way to do so.

But look at this list of matches: My father loved travel and adventure, and so do I. My father had a profound interest in nature and healing and in esoteric knowledge, and so do I. My father did not like taking orders from anyone, and neither do I. My father formed an organization of people devoted to making the world a better place, and so have I.

By the time I noticed that I had visited every country my father had ever mentioned being in, I was starting to feel like a clone. But then I took some time to think of all the things I've done that he never did, and all the places I've been where he never went, and all the goals I have that differ from his, and I realized that, although his influence was strong, his ways did not govern mine.

The Transmogrification Syndrome

Transmogrify is an odd English word meaning "to change appearance or form," and a *syndrome* is a set of behaviors often used in relation to illness. As I use the term, "Transmogrification Syndrome" refers to a curious phenomenon that often occurs when adult children visit their parents. At that time, an amazing transformation takes place as previously competent adults transmogrify into incompetent little children. And this syndrome may appear in spite of the most determined effort on the part of the adult children not to let it happen.

Actually, the experience is due to another effect called *entrainment*. When your subconscious encounters a situation in which it doesn't know what else to do, it follows habit. And when other factors—such as parents—have a strong expectation that the habitual behavior will be followed, the urge to do so is almost irresistible. In other words, if your parents expect you to behave as you did when you were completely under their domination, you probably will behave that way if you don't know what else to do.

Some adult children, upon discovering that the syndrome is taking effect, will try to use logic to avert it (the "If you haven't noticed, I'm an adult now" technique), but that doesn't work very well, because typical parents don't even hear you when you talk like that. Still other adult children will become upset and throw tantrums, but that only compounds the problem by proving that the parents are right. There is something very effective that adult children can do to avoid this problem, but it has to be done before they go home.

How to heal the Transmogrification Syndrome. The key phrase above was "if you don't know what else to do." The Transmogrification Syndrome occurs when adults have not learned a new set of behaviors to apply when their parents expect them to act like the children they once were. A long-term solution is to develop such a solid sense of self-confidence that you do not become entrained into the old behavior. A faster solution is to rehearse.

1. Think of yourself as the competent adult that you now are (or imagine yourself as the competent adult you would like to be, if the former thought doesn't work).

2. Think of or imagine how you feel as a competent adult: how you move, sit, stand, and hold your body. Take enough time for this step to form a good association with the thinking and the feelings.

3. Now imagine visiting your parents and interacting with them as the competent adult you are. Imagine how you will respond to them, how you will speak, what you will say, and how you will act. Maintain a sense of competent adult-body movement and posture the whole time.

4. After rehearsing this scenario several times, visit your parents in actuality. Do your best not to resist their attempts to behave toward you in the old way. Instead,

just maintain your competent adult way of thinking, feeling, and moving.

5. Your parents may experience some confusion at first when your old pattern doesn't emerge, but if you are persistent they will adapt to your new persona. If the results of the first visit are not satisfactory, rehearse some more.

Abusive Parents

Abuse is an unpleasant subject, but a chapter on family relationships wouldn't be complete without it. Children may be abused by family members other than parents, of course, but we'll speak in terms of parents and you can modify the focus for other relationships. Childhood abuse can take several forms, as discussed below.

Verbal abuse. This topic and solutions for it have been covered fairly well in chapter 2 on Criticism and Praise.

Physical abuse. In my opinion, modern attitudes about parental physical abuse of children have gone overboard. There is a vast difference between soundly spanking a child for breaking important rules and beating a child to the point of injury out of anger or arrogance. My father told me of hard whippings he received from his father, and my father didn't seem to have any serious emotional consequences as a result. Both my father and my mother spanked me when I deserved it (and my mother was sometimes pretty angry at the time), and I turned out okay. My own children got their share of spankings when I couldn't think of any other way to change their behavior, and all of them have turned out wonderfully (they don't spank their children, though).

The difference, I think, is whether or not the spanking is accompanied by emotional rejection. I didn't spank my children often, and it was always as a last resort for behavior change; but, when I did, I always let them know beforehand what rules had been broken, and I always assured them of my love afterward. If I had known then what I know now about human behavior, spanking would not have been necessary. But my point is that, in the context of a loving family, it did no harm.

That said, let's turn to the problem of genuine physical abuse, the kind that causes serious injury and emotional trauma. Since this is a book on relationships, the primary concern here is with the residual effects of the memories of such abuse and how it affects current relationships. The two main reactions people have to severe childhood abuse are fear and anger. The two main effects that people have from *memories* of this abuse are fear of or anger toward people of the same sex as the abuser. This happens because one of the talents of our subconscious is that of generalizing specific experiences.

As part of our survival programming, we have the ability to learn a pattern of behavior in relation to one experience and apply that learning to other, similar experiences. By getting our fingers burnt in one fire, we learn how not to touch other fires. By getting hurt by a father or mother, we learn to avoid men or women who remind us of them.

Except that it's not that simple. Being human, we may get curious about fire in general and learn how to use it or even walk on it. And the experience of getting hurt by a parent may lead us into finding ways of healing such people. Also, if the hurtful parent is the only source of love we have, we may subconsciously seek out such people, rather than avoid them. Human beings are very interesting.

Curiously, the lower a person's self-esteem, the more likely he or she is to be subconsciously attracted to people with the same characteristics as the abusing parent; and the higher a person's self-esteem, the more likely he or she is to be subconsciously *and* consciously attracted to someone with characteristics opposite those of the abuser.

If you find yourself attracted to people who turn out to be abusers, you might try raising your self-esteem with some of the ideas and techniques already given.

If your problem is that you fear entering a new relationship because the person might turn out to be just like your father or mother, here is something you can try:

1. Bring up a memory of an abusive parent, but imagine projecting it on a movie screen or seeing it as a photograph so that you don't get emotionally involved.

2. Tell yourself strongly, "This was my abusive parent, _____ (give the name if you can), a unique individual, different from any other human being on earth."

3. Continue with, "No one else I have ever known, or know now, or will ever know in the future is the same person as that person was."

4. Continue with, "That was then and this is now. I will look at new relationships as what they really are—new relationships."

5. Repeat these steps until this way of thinking feels natural or comfortable.

Emotional abuse. Some parents are simply monsters, people without compassion who either delight in torturing their own children by making them fearful, or they try to put their children into a mold that doesn't suit them, against their will and for the emotional satisfaction of the parent only.

When I was in junior high school, there was an unhappy boy who looked like a miniature body builder. He was strong and athletic and a pretty nice guy, but his father wouldn't let him socialize beyond the minimum necessary in school. His daily routine would put many athletes to shame, and he had no time just to be a boy. I don't know what happened to him, except that he never became the star his father wanted him to be.

On the side of pure terror, I know of children whose parents forced them to participate in very scary rituals that left them in a state of near-constant panic as adults. These adults have their parents almost constantly in mind, along with feelings of fear or anger. Naturally, this effect interferes with having normal adult relationships. For this problem, I am going to give you one form of the Dynamind Technique from my book, *Healing for the Millions*:

1. Hold your hands in front of you, with fingertips touching each other.

2. Think of your parent and locate the place in your body where you feel the fear or the anger.

3. Make the following statement to yourself: "When I think of my parent, I feel fear/anger in my _____ (name the place in the body). And that can change. I want that feeling to go away."

4. Each for seven times, tap the center of your chest, the top of the web of each hand between your thumb and forefinger, and the base of the back of your neck.

5. Inhale with your attention above the crown of your head, and exhale with your attention below your feet.

6. Think of your parent again, and notice if there is any change in your feelings of fear or anger. If there still is some, repeat the process.

On this same subject, at times a person may feel emotionally abused but without just cause. One of my clients felt betrayed by his mother because she left home when he was a child, and this feeling interfered with his adult life because he was afraid of being betrayed by another woman. For this problem we used a technique I call a "Skinny Description":

1. Think of a situation about which you have strong negative feelings.

2. Change your description of the situation by stating the bare facts, without any adjectives or adverbs.

3. Notice how this process changes your feelings. In the above case, the man's first description was, "My mother

betrayed me." The Skinny Description of this event was, "My mother left home and I don't know why." This changed his feelings so dramatically that he felt free of the memory for the first time.

Sexual Abuse. It is scary to think of how much sexual abuse occurs in families. At any rate, it seems like a lot when you are engaged in helping people with their emotional problems. There may even be more abuse than most people realize, because in addition to those who seek help, many others would never dream of talking about it and still others recover from it on their own.

For changing one's feelings about the experience and becoming free of its influence, some of the techniques already discussed will be helpful, including those related to forgiveness and self-esteem. Additionally, the following technique may be useful.

This technique is based on a private session in which a client asked me to play the role of her father for a few minutes. There was no dialogue at all, because most of the action was going on in her mind. We were in chairs facing each other when, to my surprise, she asked me to put my hand on her leg. When I did, she lifted it off and pushed it away. We repeated the process three times; then she sighed and smiled and told me the problem was resolved. During the process, in her mind she was encountering her father at a time when he made sexual advances. As a child she did not resist him, but as an adult she was able to rewrite the memory by imagining that, as a child, she had been able to push his hand away and refuse his overtures. The repetition and the physical presence of my hand helped to make the new memory stronger than the old, and her feelings about herself and the incident changed for the better.

1. Recall an incident of sexual abuse.

2. Imagine that you had the will and the power to refuse the advance or change the situation, and do it, vividly, in your mind.

3. Use some kind of physical movement and/or a physical prop to help reinforce your imagination.

4. Repeat the process as often as it takes to produce a change in your feelings, and every time the old memory pops up, replace it with the new memory.

HOW TO HANDLE SIBLINGS, AUNTS, UNCLES, AND COUSINS

This may be the shortest section in the book. The best way to handle these relationships is to use the same techniques discussed in this and previous chapters, as well as in the next one.

Chapter 8

Friends and Friendship

Y ou will only have two, or at most a few, parents in your life, plus a few more significant authority figures, and your other relatives may or may not be more numerous. In most cases, though, the greatest number of significant relationships in your life will be with friends.

WHAT IS A FRIEND?

Some time ago a person with whom I was discussing friendship told me that she was very selective about whom she allowed into her circle of friends, and so she had very few of them. Although she seemed proud of the fact, I said to her, "That's too bad. I have thousands of friends all over the world because I'm not selective at all."

We each have the right to determine for ourselves who our friends will be and what constitutes a friend in the first place. Since I am committed to increasing love on the planet, I am admittedly biased toward increasing friendship, rather than restricting it. So, what follows are some of my basic ideas about the subject, drawing on quotes from the Bible and Hawaiian words for related ideas. In the Book of John (15:13) for example, Jesus makes this profound statement: "Greater love hath no man than this, that a man lay down his life for his friends." This statement has become so familiar that it's easy to miss what Jesus is really saying (i.e., that there is no greater kind of love than that of friendship). It's not brotherly, or sisterly, or parental, or devotional, or altruistic love. Friendship tops them all. The rest of the biblical chapter contains equally important and related but seldom quoted statements. Here's the whole thing:

> This is my commandment, that ye love one another as I have loved you. Greater love has no man than this, that a man lay down his life for his friends. Ye are my friends. . . . Henceforth, I call you not servants, for the servant knoweth not what his lord doeth; but I have called you friends, for all things that I have heard of my father I have made known unto you.

The highest form of love that Jesus can offer his disciples is a relationship of equals. It is also worth noting that at other times when Jesus greets someone, even Judas, it is as "friend." Never as "brother" or "sister," for instance. As a matter of fact, Proverbs 17:17 says, "A friend loveth at all times, and a brother is born for adversity." Of course, if a brother is also a friend, that changes everything.

Turning again to the Bible, Exodus 33:11 says, "And the Lord spake unto Moses face to face, as a man speaketh unto his friend." And the Book of James (2:23) says that Abraham was called the "Friend of God." Obviously this term was used on purpose to convey a very high kind of mutual love.

Nor do friends have to be people. Some studies show that people with pets tend to be not only happier but healthier, too. Is there a difference between friendship and love? Apparently not. In Middle English the word *friend* means "lover," and it stems from a word in Old Gothic meaning "to love." If anything, it implies a deeper kind of love, one that goes beyond obligation.

In English, the degree of closeness of a friendship can only be suggested by adjectives, such as a "fair-weather friend," a "close friend," an "intimate friend." The Hawaiian language has many separate words for *friend* to signify varying degrees and types of friendship. *Hoaloha* (beloved companion), for example, is a general term for friend. *Makamaka* (face to face) is a friend with whom you share freely. *Aikane* (a word of uncertain derivation) is a close, personal friend of the same sex. *Pilialoha* (sticky love) is a romantic friend. And here's a great one: *'au ko'i* (axe handle), which refers to a trusted friend.

Ralph Waldo Emerson said, "The only way to have a friend is to be one." But many people have trouble making friends because they don't know how to be one. So here is a set of guidelines to help you remember, based on the letters of the English word *friend*. The letters may not apply in other languages, but the concepts do.

F STANDS FOR FREEDOM

Friends do not try to control each other. I have encountered many people, clients, and students who have personal relationships they call "friendships," but which sound more like parent/child relationships when they are described. The need or desire for control comes from a need or desire for power over the other person. And this desire, of course, comes from a fear of being powerless.

One person in a close relationship may try to control the other's behavior in many ways, but the most common is through direct or indirect criticism.

Direct criticism is simply that: verbal statements that criticize another person's behavior. Often disguised euphemistically as "constructive" (i.e., "I'm pretending to do this for your own good, but I'm really doing it so that you will do what I want you to do"), frequent direct criticism is destructive to the relationship and to the self-esteem of the person on the receiving end. Below are some techniques for neutralizing the effect of such criticism and discouraging its use. None of them are confrontational, but they will probably require practice to be effective:

Anti-Criticism Technique #1: Self-Compliments

This technique helps you relieve the tension caused by the other person's criticism.

It is one of those deceptively simple exercises that can produce dramatic results: Whenever you receive a direct criticism, mentally give yourself a compliment. The compliment does not have to be related to the criticism. It is helpful to have already compiled a short list of true compliments to give yourself—perhaps four or five—that you can memorize for such occasions.

Anti-criticism Technique #2: "Fogging"

This technique is adapted from one called "Fogging" in Manuel P. Smith's book, *When I Say No I Feel Guilty*. Fogging is especially effective when someone is trying to use criticism on you in a manipulative way, trying to make you feel guilty, or trying to get you to do something you don't want to do. I have used it many times with good results.

1. When someone criticizes you, accept any part of it you choose, but under your own terms. Let's suppose someone says, "You never do anything right!" You would reply with something like, "You're right. I do make too many mistakes." You see? You've accepted the criticism, but not as it was stated. As long as you can accept that you probably do make too many mistakes, this reply would work.

2. If someone says, "You just did a lousy job," you might reply, "You're right, I could have done better"—if indeed you can accept the idea that you could have done better. The point is to modify the criticism in a way that you can tolerate. You acknowledge your modification, not the original criticism.

This technique is called "Fogging" because it almost always leaves the person criticizing you in a fog. He knows you just did something, but he can't quite figure out what it was. You are not taking this action to make him feel that way, you're doing it to make yourself feel stronger and to handle criticism better. It's a wonderfully powerful technique, because in the process of accepting the part that you modify, you become your own judge without having to defend yourself or become stressed at the criticism. And you do not acknowledge that anyone else has the right to judge you.

Anti-criticism Technique #3: The Bamboo Technique

This one will be more difficult for some people, because it requires you to accept what the other person says *without* modification. It is particularly suitable to situations where the criticism is specific and accurate. As a technique, it greatly resembles what Smith's book calls "Negative Assertion," but I learned it as the "Bamboo Technique" from my father.

When someone criticizes you specifically and accurately, acknowledge it completely. If someone says, "You promised to take me someplace and you didn't do it. You broke your promise!" Instead of defending yourself, you would say, "Yes, I did break my promise. You have a right to feel unhappy about that." You are acknowledging the criticism and you are sympathizing with the critic. Accepting full responsibility when it is justified leaves you feeling stronger and the critic less unhappy.

You could also say "I'm sorry" and offer an explanation, but don't offer excuses.

I've had reason to use this technique a number of times in my life. On one important occasion, it had surprising aftereffects. I was in the country of Dahomey (now called Benin), working as the director of socioeconomic development programs for an American voluntary agency. My counterpart in the government was the director of social services, whom I'll call Mr. P. Our relationship to this point had been one of wary acquaintances. One morning he called me to say that the minister of health required our presence immediately.

No explanation was given, so I hurried to the minister's office only to find that Mr. P. had arranged the meeting for the purpose of criticizing my actions and getting me into trouble with the minister. As I listened to Mr. P.'s litany of accusations, I remembered my father telling me that an oak tree stands firm and resists the wind, but if the wind is strong enough it blows the tree over; whereas a bamboo tree bends with the wind no matter how strong it is, and when the wind stops the bamboo hasn't changed position at all.

When Mr. P.'s wind stopped, I looked the minister in the eye and said, "Mr. P. is absolutely correct. I did every one of those things. May I tell you my purpose in doing them?" When the minister nodded I gave a point-by-point explanation—not an excuse—for each action.

Before I was finished, Mr. P. threw up his hands in a dramatic gesture and said, "You see! You see, Mr. Minister. The man is like smoke! You can't grab hold of him!" The minister laughed and dismissed us both. In the corridor, Mr. P. did something totally unexpected. He invited me out for a drink, and that was the beginning of a wary friendship.

CHAPTER 8

Handling Indirect Criticism

As opposed to direct criticism, indirect criticism is more subtly manipulative and difficult to deal with, because disapproval is conveyed not through words but by gesture, facial expression, and a myriad of behavior patterns that convey the critic's unhappiness with you. The subtlety makes the situation hard to counteract, because our natural impulse to be liked and to cooperate with others is so strong. Even worse, a person with low self-esteem may have a tendency to interpret another person's behavior as critical even when it is not. What works best in this case is purposeful, ongoing practices that increase self-esteem. When self-esteem is high enough, indirect criticism ceases to have any effect.

R STANDS FOR RESPECT

In the previous chapter, I mentioned the need for respect regarding children, and the same thing applies to friends. My particular concern here is respect for differences. Friends don't have to be clones. Of course, for there to be a friendship at all there must be shared beliefs, values, and interests, but there can also be different beliefs, different values, and different interests. I have some great friends who don't believe in Huna, aren't interested in shamanism, don't care for Hawaii, and would rather have a beer than make the world a better place. But they like me and I like them and we have a good time together, because of what we *do* share.

Sometimes, in the course of a friendship, people take very different life paths. This often results in much less personal contact, but it doesn't have to mean an end to the friendship. There are friends I haven't seen or heard from in over twenty years, yet I know that if we met again it would be a delightful experience. Friends don't always have to stay in your neighborhood.

Over the course of my life, I have occasionally lost respect for a person I once considered my friend. In every case the person had acted in a way that is contrary to one of my core values. Everyone has a set of core values—ideas, concepts, behaviors, expectations—that are so fundamental they define our deepest sense of right and wrong, good and bad, important and unimportant. We have lesser values that define the same things, but the core values are more powerful and more difficult to change. We feel the most rapport with people who share one or more of our core values without going against the rest, and the least rapport with people whose values or behavior go against one or more of our core values. Most people I've met don't even think about such things; yet their core values guide their life and their friendships, regardless.

A Core Value Exercise

The more aware you are of your own core values, the more you will understand your own behavior and your relationships with the people around you.

1. Make a list of up to ten things for which you would give your life, or for which you would change your life.

2. Imagine a few situations in which such things might happen, and note how you feel about them.

3. Try to reduce each thing to a single sentence or keyword.

I Stands for Independence

A friend is someone on whom you can depend for something, according to the closeness or depth of the friendship. You might be able to depend on a casual friend for good conversation and an intimate friend for help in the most dire situation you might ever experience. At the same time, it is not healthy for either of you to be too dependent on each other. You know that too much dependency is involved when you cannot feel happy, competent, or whole without the presence of your friend. This kind of situation signals that the relationship has devolved from friendship into an addictive relationship based on a need for love and for power. In such a relationship, one or both people might be stuck in dependency. In either case, it's a great strain on both, because the happiness that is supposed to be part of friendship is missing.

A Disengagement Technique

If you are the independent one in a relationship, here is something you can do to disengage gently. This exercise uses mind-to-mind communication:

1. Imagine some kind of space in which you feel comfortable, outdoors or indoors. Take some time to see and hear and feel details.

2. Mentally invite the person from whom you wish to disengage into your space, and arrange things for a conversation. Let the person know that it is time to change the relationship and that greater happiness awaits the person elsewhere. Imagine that the other person receives this communication with understanding.

3. After talking, open a door or gate leading out of your space and onto a path that goes toward a bright light or a beautiful valley or a happy group of people. Imagine the person leaving your space and reaching the other destination.

4. Repeat this exercise daily until the relationship begins to change.

An Independence Technique

On the other hand, if you are the *dependent* one in a relationship and want to get free of your addiction, this exercise will be helpful:

1. Imagine a space in which you are with the person from whom you are seeking independence. Say goodbye and walk away. If this is difficult for any reason, such as because of emotional or physical reactions, walk away just as far as you can without distress.

2. Repeat this exercise daily, and keep increasing the distance by small amounts until you can comfortably walk away and out of sight without needing to go back.

E Stands for Equality

There is no hierarchy in a friendship. Sometimes people who are in a hierarchy—social, governmental, military, religious, or whatever—do become friends with someone at a different level than they are, but the hierarchy and the friendship cannot coexist simultaneously. When the hierarchy is active, the friendship is lessened, and when the friendship is active, the hierarchy is lessened. Some people can work with this alternation of roles, but for others it is too much of a strain. A king may make friends with a commoner during a hunt, but the friendship dissolves at the palace. A captain may make friends with a private during a battle, but they can't mix socially at the base. A high priest can be friends with an acolyte, but the friendship cannot be expressed in the church or the temple.

When people get together in unorganized groups of two or more, it is natural for an informal hierarchy of leaders and followers to develop. With friends, however, this informal hierarchy is constantly shifting. This can be easily observed at a party where people exchange roles as they tell stories or lead activities. If you are in a relationship with one or more people where one person is always in charge, then, although the relationship might be friendly, it is not a relationship of friends.

N STANDS FOR NURTURE

To nurture a friend is to provide support and encouragement for that person's growth and development. This could take the form of physical, emotional, mental, financial, or social support, depending on the nature of the friendship and the capabilities of the friends. Encouragement that promotes a friend's growth and development, though, can be given under any circumstances. When you are with a friend, it's simply a matter of expressing your encouragement with the appropriate words and gestures. When you are separated from your friend for the time being, you can still help in a different way, using the concept that you are always connected through your spirit.

How to Bless a Distant Friend

This kind of nurturing is what I call a blessing. By my definition that means an energized focus on something your friend wants or needs. It can be done at any time, but I like to bless my friends in the morning soon after I get up. Here is one way to do it:

1. Look at something beautiful to harmonize your own energy, and then think of your friend.

2. Imagine your friend surrounded by a field of energy— perhaps in the form of a bright, colored light or some beautiful music.

3. Mentally state your blessing as specifically as is practical. The thing to remember is always to bless a good thing

that you want to strengthen or increase. So, you could say, "I bless your health, happiness, and success today." Or, if there is a more specific need or desire, you could say something like, "I bless the success of your job interview."

D STANDS FOR DEVOTION

A devoted friend is one who is loyal and helpful whenever, wherever, and for as long as he or she is able to be. A devoted friend would not use friendship as an excuse to try to make someone do something contrary to what that person believes is good and right. Many people cite friendship as their reason for doing something that contradicts their core values, when actually they do it out of fear of being criticized for "not being a friend." Friends do not get their friends into trouble or put them in harm's way for selfish purposes.

Devoted friends are also forgiving. Forgiveness is a vitally important topic for all kinds of relationships. If you like, reread chapter 3 on forgiveness with friendship in mind.

The Hawaiians make such an art of making friends that I'll end this chapter with one of their proverbs describing a good friendship:

Pili kau, pili ho'oilo.
Together in the dry season, together in the wet season.

Chapter 9

Lovers and Spouses

The title of this chapter is not meant to imply that lovers can't be spouses, or that spouses can't be lovers. Of course they can! Except when they can't. Also, the word *lover* in this chapter may refer to any type of romantic relationship and the word *spouse* to any type of domestic partnership—although my comments may be biased toward relationships between a man and a woman. In addition to whatever I say below, both lovers and spouses could benefit from studying the previous section on self-esteem and chapter 8 on Friends and Friendship.

When we describe two people as being *lovers* in the English language, the implication is strong that they are having sex together. If we say they are "in love," then the range of relationship possibilities expands considerably, because people in love aren't necessarily lovers. Curious, isn't it? In any case, in this section on "lovers" I'm going to talk about different kinds of relationships of people "in love."

CHAPTER 9

THAT URGE

The urge to move toward a closer, more physically intimate relationship with another person begins around puberty, when hormones are changing and bodies are preparing for making and bearing children. For some reason, human beings are designed, intelligently or not, to get an extraordinary amount of pleasure from the sexual act and all the activities leading up to it. The fact that they often don't is not the fault of the designer. Religious and cultural beliefs and practices are most responsible for that.

In addition to the pleasure of the act, the urge to connect with someone with whom to engage in it is incredibly powerful and influences a great deal of human behavior. Beliefs about it, however, can distort much of that behavior. So can suppressed knowledge about it.

I recall a Charlie Brown cartoon in which the littlest kid, Linus, tells his sister about a cute little girl he found attractive on his first day of school.

"Did you talk to her?" asked Lucy.
"No," said Linus.
"Then what did you do?"
"I hit her!"

Linus's response is funny because so many people can relate to it. For the most part, people are taught very little about how to behave when they feel attracted to another person, and so they often do weird things, even as adults. Part of the problem is certainly physiological, though, because sometimes the urge can be so strong that it clouds good judgment. Here's one version of the problem from my novel, *Dangerous Journeys*, in which two women are sharing a joke:

> After God made man, he said to the new creature, "I have given you the means to have dominion over the earth and to go forth and multiply, but there's a little problem."
> "What's the problem?" asked the man.
> "Well, to do that I had to endow you with a brain and a penis," said God.
> "What could be wrong with that?" queried the man.
> God looked embarrassed. "The problem is that they don't ever work at the same time."

Men, and probably women, too, understand the problem very well. I recently read a news report about a newly-wed female schoolteacher who started a love affair with a fourteen-year-old boy during a class outing, so it is not only a male problem. I don't have a solution, except to say that if adolescents were taught the emotional and mental as well as the physical effects of the "Urge" it might be helpful. So might training in self-esteem and in thinking about the consequences of one's actions.

And acting on that attractive urge isn't always a problem. I also read recently about a couple who eloped to get married when the girl was fourteen and the boy was seventeen. Family and friends were all against it, and everyone predicted it couldn't last. The article was featuring their seventieth wedding anniversary, and both of them were still very much in love.

How to Know When You're in Love

How to recognize being in love is very confusing for many people, because of the close links between sexual and other attractions. Let's explore the things that attract people to each other.

Sexual Attraction

From the viewpoint of each individual, some people are more sexually attractive than others. There are those who think that sexual attraction has to do with how beautiful or handsome someone is, but that isn't necessarily so. Everyone is attracted to beauty as they define it, but that perception is primarily culturally based. Remember the Dassantch of Ethiopia and their "cattle cosmetics" in chapter 4? Good looks, cosmetics, clothing, and jewelry are used to attract attention, but all they do is give sexual attraction an opportunity to occur.

People have many motivations for having sex—including political, economic, social, emotional, and mental—and many ways of stimulating their own sexual-energy level, but sexual attraction between two people is awakened by a certain energetic resonance. Within our personal energy fields, each of us has a particular sexual frequency, vibrating quietly or strongly at any given moment and sending waves out into our environment. When we encounter someone else whose sexual-frequency waves are in some degree of harmonic resonance with our own, the level of energy is amplified for both. The amplification may be mild, as when we find ourselves slightly turned on by someone at a party, or it can be wild, like the ninety-foot rogue waves that sometimes form at sea when two waves from different storms meet at exactly the same place at the same time.

I once had such an incident with a complete stranger when attending an organized healing circle a long time ago. I was seated between a man on my left and a reasonably attractive woman on my right. I didn't know or speak to either of them. When it came time to start we held hands, and the moment my hand touched the woman's I was overwhelmed by an incredible surge of sexual energy, accompanied by a vivid vision of the two of us making love. I think it only lasted a few seconds, because my attention was brought back to the room by the man on my left, who said in a startled voice, "What was that?" When I asked what he meant, he said that he felt a wave of energy rushing across his lap. When I glanced at the woman, she looked shaken, but we didn't speak to each other. Even later, during the socializing, it was evident that we were both feeling something for each other. I was, shall we say, not thinking with my brain and gave serious consideration to getting together with her. Fortunately, that night I had a vivid dream in which I was shown the negative consequences of such behavior, and I never made contact with her again. Nor did she try to contact me.

The point is that strong sexual attraction can happen any time, anywhere, but that doesn't mean you are supposed to do anything about it. It's just an energy effect. People who are strongly sexually attracted to each other may have great sex, but they may not have anything else in common, and they may not even like each other.

Once in a while, during a workshop presentation a woman may tell me that she feels a strong sexual attraction for me. Sometimes it really is a sexual attraction, because I feel it, too, but more often it is her interpretation of the excitement she felt from what I call my "workshop energy." In either case, I use the below RTS technique to keep things calm. Naturally, you have to make your own choices about what to do when sexual attraction occurs, but if you don't want to do anything then this technique can help.

The RTS Technique

This technique came from an experience I had on Kauai when my friend and colleague Susan and I were waiting on a street corner for my wife, Gloria, to pick us up. Susan bought an ice cream cone and offered me some. At the time, Gloria and I were experimenting with a very strict diet that definitely did not include ice cream. Nevertheless, it was a hot day, so I took one lick. A few moments later, Susan offered me another taste and I politely refused.

"How can you not take another bite of this delicious ice cream?" she asked, astonished.

"Simple," I told her, "I'm keeping my shoulders so relaxed that I can't lift my arms to hold the cone."

So, RTS stands for "relax the shoulders." It works well both for diets and for when someone offers you a tempting sexual experience and you don't want to get involved. Keep your shoulders so relaxed that you can't lift your arms, and you'll be less like to get into trouble. And if the other person claims to be having sexual fantasies about me, I say, "Great, enjoy them!"

Emotional Attraction

Emotional attraction is not the same as sexual attraction, but the two of them together make for wonderful loving. Emotional attraction is also what keeps good friends together, and it is the reason why good lovers can also be good friends, but good friends don't have to be lovers.

The specific emotion involved is simple happiness. Energetically, it works much like sexual attraction, in that when you are in the right harmonic resonance with someone, their presence—or even just the thought of them—makes you feel happy.

At this point I want to lay aside a myth that is too often promoted by poets, novelists, movies, and musical lyrics: the myth that love is painful. In one movie I saw, the heroine punches the hero hard enough for him to complain and says, "Love hurts." Then she kisses him. Many people relate to that because they've accepted the myth. Songs talk about the "heartbreak of love," and novels describe love as a state in which the mind spins, the heart throbs, the stomach is full of butterflies, and the knees tremble, which sounds more like vitamin deficiency to me. Many people actually believe that jealousy, heartache, anxiety, and sadness are signs of love, and they even measure the love in a relationship by the presence of those feelings.

Let's wake up, folks! That is all a *distortion* of love, fostered by people who don't know how to love. The essence of love is feeling good. Even *Webster's Encyclopedic Unabridged Dictionary of the English Language* has only good things to say about love, and it emphasizes the affection aspect of it. My preference, of course, is for the Hawaiian definition found in the word *aloha*. As a word it contains meanings of love, affection, compassion, mercy, sympathy, kindness, charity, and greeting. In its roots, *alo* means "presence," or "one who is esteemed," and *oha* means "affection," "love," "greeting," and "to show joyous affection or friendship." Here, too, good feeling predominates as a characteristic of love.

When two people like each other their auras act like attracting magnets. It is not easy to see the energy, but it is very easy to see and experience the effect. In some of my workshops I demonstrate this by inviting to the stage two people who have declared that they like each other very much. It doesn't matter whether they are men or women or couples or friends. When they are on the stage I have them stand back to back about a foot (30 cm) apart, and then I have them think about how much they enjoy each others' company. Invariably, when they have the kind of relationship that makes them happy together, they will be drawn backward toward each other until their backs collide, without any conscious effort. Next time you are walking with someone you like, pay attention to how often you seemingly inadvertently brush up against or bump into each other. That is emotional attraction at work.

Mental Attraction

Mental attraction is much more subtle than either sexual or emotional attraction, but the energetic structure is the same. Not only do "great minds think alike," as the proverb goes, they attract each other, too.

While sexual and emotional attraction are enough for short-term or occasional love affairs, long-term loving also requires some mental rapport. Even long-term friendships require some mental rapport, a certain number of shared ideas, beliefs, and values. In fact, some friendships exist by mental resonance only, but that's not enough for lovers.

Two people do not have to agree about all their ideas, beliefs, and values, but the more basic concurrence there is, the more creative and intellectually stimulating the relationship will be. My wife and I are friends first, lovers second, and spouses third. Our strong, mutual mental attraction enhances all three forms of relationship, and we provide creative stimulation for each other in many ways. However, if I try to discuss philosophy with her she falls asleep; if I try to tell her about my latest computer game she gets a blank look on her face; if I try to interest her in the fine points of Hawaiian grammar she finds something else to do. On the other hand, if she tries to involve me in shopping I find a place to sit and wait for her; if she tries to discuss the fine points of biometrics for the elderly my eyes glaze over; if she wants to look at houses I find something else to do (that doesn't always work, though). Still, we have enough areas of rapport that the areas where we *lack* rapport don't matter in terms of how we relate. When we want to do those things, we either do them alone or find someone else to do them with.

Spiritual Attraction

To tell the truth, I have mixed feelings about the issue of spiritual attraction. To tell the whole truth, I find that a lot of other people do, too. The problem arises, of course, because of all the different ideas people have about what the word *spiritual* means. Some people think of it in terms of "finding a soul mate." For those of you who don't know, one version of this theory is that in the form of spirit we are whole, but as we are conceived we split into two souls, and the purpose of life is to find your "twin soul" and automatically join together in blissful harmony. Well, hey, if that works for you, fine. It seems to me, though, that it's not a very efficient system, because the world appears to have too many souls who are not able to find each other. I also became a little skeptical of this theory when a spiritual teacher I knew announced to the world that he had found his soul mate and married her shortly after. A few years later they divorced, and the teacher announced to the world that he had found his "new" soul mate. Go figure.

Another version of the theory says that for every person in the world there is one perfect person who is destined to be your soul mate, and if you can find him or her you will discover how blissful love can be. I know people who spend their lives searching for this perfect person, and while they look they avoid committing to anyone else, even when the sexual, emotional, and mental attractions are good, because the one they are with isn't perfect. And all the ones I know who have followed this theory are fundamentally unhappy. This is not surprising when you consider how much time they must spend negatively comparing the person at hand with their ideal. If they could take the attitude of the leprechaun in the play and movie *Finian's Rainbow*, they could be much happier: "When I'm not near the girl I love, I love the girl I'm near."

Another way of looking at spiritual attraction is in terms of telepathic attraction. In this theory, if you focus and affirm and visualize the kind of person you want, then he or she will be magnetically attracted to you by your telepathic broadcast. Here's how you do it:

1. List the qualities you want in a soul mate (or a lover or spouse). Add pictures and symbols to represent those qualities.

2. Sit quietly and make a statement affirming that this person will come, or is coming, into your life right now.

3. Imagine the two of you enjoying life together.

The good news is that this technique usually works, if you can eliminate enough of your fears and doubts. The bad news is twofold: a) the person will not always have all the qualities on your list and will always have some qualities *not* on your list—whether the mix works for you depends on how flexible you are; and b) when the person does come into your life, he or she may not want to *stay* there. The factor here is whether you are the kind of person the other one would want to be with.

It's amazing to me how many people ignore this side of the relationship equation. They make a long list of rules and conditions for the kind of person they want to attract and do nothing to be the kind of person that would attract the person they want. I suggest that people who want to try this technique give it some thought and list the changes they could make in their own thinking, behavior, and appearance in order for it to work.

Then there's the "no accident" theory to which I ascribe. I tend toward the idea that Spirit gives us opportunities to meet possible friends, lovers, and spouses who resonate with our energy patterns and potentials at given moments in our life. In that sense, they are spiritually attracted to us. Then, however, it's up to us to do something about it, and that's where the hard work of relating comes in. When I first met my wife we were instantly attracted on several levels. In the course of our seven-year courtship, however, there were many occasions when we each came close to leaving and following another path, and each time we decided not to.

Now, some people would call that proof of our being fated for each other, but I do not believe in such fate. We did not stay together under the compulsion of destiny, we stayed together because of choices we made of our own free will.

I will not speak for my wife, but here are two experiences from my side. The first was at a time when it felt to me that we were within a hair's breadth of splitting up. Then I made the choice not to give up.

"I will end up marrying you no matter how long it takes, no matter what you do," I told her. "I will not give up even when you are walking down the aisle with another man. Even if you get married to someone else, I will not give up."

That declaration sounds a little extreme now, I admit, but I made it during a passionate moment.

The second time was just before I finished my military service. A friend of mine and I were planning a sailing voyage through the South Pacific when we got out. It was a serious venture and I was excited about it. Then the time of choice came. Do I go on this great adventure of a lifetime, or do I go home and continue wooing the woman I love? There was no guarantee that the adventure would be successful, although there was no doubt that it would be an adventure. There was no guarantee that my wooing would be successful, either, and no doubt that it would be difficult.

Nevertheless, when the time came to choose, I took the greater risk and went home to woo—which turned out to be the best possible choice I could have made and an even greater adventure than the one I had planned.

My main point here is that loving relationships do not just happen. Their continuance is based on daily choices of how to act and how to react, on daily decisions about what it important and what is not important. And if you think it's hard to be lovers, just wait until you get married.

CHAPTER 9

SPOUSES

Marriage is a curious cultural phenomenon. Some form of it occurs everywhere in human societies. Originally, it was probably the result of emotional bonding that occurred after, or during, sexual attraction. Later, it became the focus of a family group for the rearing of children and economic security. At some point, marriage became important enough to be a cause for celebration, or to be part of a more general celebration to ensure the fertility of the social group and/or the land. The link between the fertility of humans and the fertility of the land was very important in ancient Europe, but not in Hawaii. Humans and elemental gods each took care of their own fertility in ancient Polynesia.

In the temperate zones of the planet, springtime, when plants and animals give birth to new life, became the primary time for nuptials. In the tropical climate of Hawaii, where there is no specific season of spring, formal marriage was typically held on the eleventh night of the moon, called *Huna*. In the roots of this word are references to male and female energy.

In time, societal leaders in many parts of the world—and even commoners, in some places—began to appreciate the political benefits of marriage as a means of bonding family and tribal groups. The legal aspects of marriage, involving bride price, dowries, the sharing of property, and inheritance probably began at this time. Religious involvement in marriage for people in general came quite late in the Western world. Of course, religions got involved in the marriages of politically important people very early. But it was not until the twelfth century AD that the European Christian church even acknowledged marriage among commoners and centuries later before it became a sacrament.

Marriage in our modern times is in a very confused state. Governments have taken control of it because of its economic impact on society. Religious involvement continues only as a matter of individual belief and in those areas where religions have political power. Engaging in multiple marriages at the same time is outlawed in most places, but, especially in Western nations, serial marriages (one after the other) are common, and divorce—a process far more difficult than marriage because of economic considerations—has become a major industry. In addition, the very definition of marriage as a union between a man and a woman has come into question.

In spite of such complications, from the time the custom began until now the fundamental factor in any sort of marriage has been the ability of two individuals to join harmoniously in a commitment to form an enduring relationship. I am not concerned in this book with the purpose of marriage. It doesn't matter if the marriage is based on politics, economics, convenience, rearing children, or profound love, it still involves two people who have to find some way to get along with each other. It doesn't even matter if it's a multiple marriage; there will still be two people in the group who have to get along. Nor does it matter whether the couple is composed of a man and a woman, two women, or two men, because the same concepts apply. In what follows, I am arbitrarily making several assumptions:

- A couple of people in an enduring, live-in relationship want to get along better, or at least one of them does.

- Ideas and techniques from previous chapters also apply to spousal relationships, so I won't repeat them.

- The ideas and techniques presented may apply to anyone, even if I use male/female examples or talk about marriage as the relationship.

Who Is This Person, Anyway?

Some people get married within a few days or weeks of meeting, so it is hardly surprising when difficulties arise as they discover things they didn't know about each other. Everyone of marriageable age has already developed a variety of habits, predilections, and idiosyncrasies that may not be compatible with a mate. Didn't you know that your spouse liked to nibble on snacks in bed? That he or she couldn't sleep unless the room was very hot or very cold? That he couldn't stand broccoli? That she didn't know how to cook? That he dropped his underwear on the floor? That she would use any razor at hand to shave her legs?

There is no way to know everything about a person before a marriage, even if you've known that person or lived together for a long time. Gloria and I had known each other for seven years before we got married and had dated for most of that time. Yet, in our first year of marriage we were in for a lot of surprises.

Right after we got married in Michigan we moved to Boulder, Colorado, where I enrolled in the university while Gloria worked in a hospital near Denver. Our first surprise together occurred when we looked for our first apartment and realized that neither of us knew what the other liked or expected in a place to live. After some discussion, we narrowed our needs to the basics. I insisted on a shower, and she insisted on a refrigerator with a freezer. When we found that combination we settled in, because anything else about the apartment that wasn't good was just an inconvenience.

A big surprise for Gloria was my choice of a major area of study for my last two years of undergraduate school. At the University of Michigan, I had been enrolled in Russian Studies. When I went to enroll in the same major at the University of Colorado, I had trouble communicating what I wanted to the head of the Russian Department (who wanted me to do what he wanted). In frustration, I appealed to the head of the Asian Studies Department, who was in charge of several different departments, to resolve the problem. Although that was the beginning of a long and fruitful friendship, I really can't remember what happened in his office. All I do know is that I came out signed up for Chinese Studies. When I went home and told Gloria, she seemed to accept it quietly, but years later she told me that she was profoundly shocked. Nobody changes his major in his junior year, she thought. Who is this man I have married?

My own big surprise took place in the bathroom. Perhaps the stress we were under of trying to balance work, schooling, and marriage explains why it affected me so much. Anyway, early one morning I suddenly noticed the toothpaste tube we shared. To my horror, Gloria had squeezed the tube in the middle to get the toothpaste out and left it that way! No one in their right mind squeezes the toothpaste tube in the *middle*. Everyone knows you're supposed to roll it up from the bottom. What kind of person had I married?

I found myself becoming very upset, but fortunately my shamanic training around the issue of anger kicked in. The process is a simple one that resembles a post-hypnotic suggestion. All you do is to become very relaxed and repeat to yourself that every time you get angry you will do something to change the anger. Changing the anger itself is more interesting. The technique I used in the bathroom was one my father had taught me called "Sitting on the Moon":

1. When some incident angers you, imagine yourself sitting on the moon and looking at the earth.

2. Let yourself realize how unimportant the incident is from that point of view.

3. Take a deep breath, go back to the incident, and handle it differently.

The method I used to handle it differently in the case of the toothpaste was the "Permission Technique," in which I grandly gave Gloria permission to squeeze the tube any way she wanted (of course I didn't tell her that at the time).

That dissipated my anger very well. Some months later, I surprised myself by discovering that I had picked up her squeezing habit.

Do It Now, Do It Later

For any couple to get along, they must share some critical core values, but each person will also have many noncritical values that can make relating irritatingly difficult at times. Our noncritical values can include a wide range of things based on such factors as how our parents did things, what we've read in books or seen in movies, and habits of likes and dislikes. In a long-term relationship, the values each person holds have numerous opportunities to bump into each other, causing various degrees of upset according to current stress levels. (At the same time, we each also have noncritical values that may not bump into anything.)

For instance, when my stress levels are up, I become irritable and snappish if I'm hungry. In my youth I frequently had to go hungry, and stress in the present brings out a subconscious fear related to those times. Fortunately, my reaction doesn't bother Gloria because she doesn't give it any importance. The fact that I'm quickly over it makes it even less important. When Gloria is under stress, on the other hand, she tends to misplace things; but that doesn't bother me because I have no values of importance attached to that kind of behavior.

When it comes to doing tasks, though, our noncritical values bump rather hard. When she wants something done, she wants it done *right now*, regardless of what I'm doing or what my plans are. And she will usually badger me until I give up and do what she wants (which could be anything from taking out the trash to repairing a shelf or washing the car). Sometimes, however, I will dig in and refuse to do it in the moment but promise to do it later (and I often keep those promises). Then she gets irritated and often does the task herself, which irritates me because she didn't wait for me to do it when I was ready. The funny thing is that we often reverse these behaviors when I want *her* to do something. Then, sometimes, *she* puts it off and *I* end up doing it (somehow, though, that doesn't bother her).

The types of values mentioned above are just examples. Every couple will have their own noncritical values that bump into each other from time to time. A problem emerges only when what people don't like about each other becomes more important than what they do like. This tends to happen when the good aspects of a relationship are taken for granted or forgotten. If that process is left unchecked, it is all too easy for excessive criticism to raise its ugly head and destroy the marriage.

What can you do about that? I can only tell you what works in my marriage and what I know has worked for many others. What Gloria and I do can simply be called "Daily Blessing." Here's how it works:

1. Shortly after we get up in the morning, we do an informal blessing ritual in which we praise all the good qualities we like about each other, give appreciation to our home and environment, and send good wishes out to all the people we care about.

2. Throughout the day we make it a point to say "Please" and "Thank you" in our dealings with each other.

3. We frequently say "I love you" during the day; kiss each other when parting, even for a little while; and always say "I love you," kiss, and wish each other good dreams at night (unless I fall asleep first). Believe me, this practice keeps all the little irritations from becoming big ones.

Mind Reading

I never knew there were so many active clairvoyants in our society until I began doing couple counseling. The trouble is, none of them are very good clairvoyants. When anyone in a relationship begins to assume that he or she knows what the other person is thinking, then communication problems are already in play. The best clairvoyants in the world can't read the other person's mind on a daily basis in a close relationship, much less untrained dabblers. When you assume you know what your partner is thinking, all you are really doing is drawing on memories of that person's previous behavior. Oh, you might be accurate sometimes in certain circumstances if you know the person well and he or she is a slave of habit, but in most cases you will be wrong because people grow and change whether you notice or not.

I was once the houseguest of a woman friend and her husband. The woman was active in metaphysical affairs, and the husband was in charge of a local government facility. Over dinner one night she happened to mention that her husband had no interest in or understanding of meta-physical things. Her husband didn't say anything. But late in the evening on a different night, he and I were alone and had a chance to get to know each other better. It turned out that he had a profound wealth of metaphysical knowledge and ideas, but because of his wife's assumption he never got to talk to her about them. As a result, she missed out on the possibility of deeper communication with her husband and even of learning from him.

The worst cases of false mind reading, as far as the mind reader is concerned, are when people imagine that their partner is angry with them, or thinking angry thoughts about them, or criticizing them—when none of that is the case. This problem has its roots in low self-esteem, and it may cause the mind reader to destroy the marriage without cause.

Almost as bad is when one partner tries to force the other to mind read. This is merely a form of manipulation, but the effects can be devastating on the person being forced and on the relationship. The situation can occur in many ways, but in every case the implication is that you are an idiot or have done something wrong if you do not know by telepathy what the other person wants or feels.

If someone expects you to know what they are think-ing based on their gestures or facial expressions alone, you have the right to say, "I don't understand what you mean." Often such a person will use the classic phrase, "If you don't know, I'm not going to tell you," which is exquisitely designed to make you feel incompetent and inadequate. If you have enough self-esteem, you can just step back and say, "No, I'm not going to read minds." It is important to learn not to be afraid of other people's gestures and expressions and to recognize them for what they really are: simply gestures and expressions. But you may need some mental practice beforehand to be able to react differently.

Express your anger—carefully. There are times in a couple's relationship when one person may get very angry at the other. The anger may be due to stress, broken rules, or something else, but it puts a great strain on relating. Couples may handle such anger in various ways, depending on the personalities involved.

Some people handle a partner's angry outburst by not taking it personally. This can work well, but it isn't common. Some people react by yelling back, which can serve as a means of communication and of letting off steam without ill effect. But this is also uncommon.

More common is the situation where one partner yells, the other yells back, and the yelling escalates until either they get into a fight, or one or both just leave the scene. In the latter case, a healthy outcome occurs when they make up, but that doesn't always happen. Most commonly, one partner gets angry but holds it in without expressing it, or the partner being yelled at gets angry but holds it in without expressing it. Either case can lead to a bigger and possibly more violent outburst from the one holding anger back or to a break-up of the relationship.

In order to learn the best way to handle anger in your relationship, pay attention to your partner's anger-related behavior. In the field of anger management, one popular therapeutic approach is to have you air your grievances so that your partner knows why you are feeling angry. Yeah, right. I hate to disappoint you, but that only works if your partner is a saint or an angel, or if he or she has such high self-esteem that they are able to hear your anger without taking it personally. Unfortunately, not many of us are married to saints or angels or people with such high self-esteem. Most people when confronted with openly expressed anger react by expressing their anger right back or by building up resentment. Even the ancient Hawaiians were smarter than that. In the family-therapy system of *ho'oponopono*, anger was allowed to be expressed only through a third, neutral, party.

The expression of anger in a relationship is always due to some kind of power issue. It happens when one of the partners is feeling powerless or that his or her power is threatened. This is why communicating anger often makes the other person angry in turn. Unless you know for sure that expressing your anger to your partner will not have any bad consequences, it is better not to do it. However, suppressing it may be just as bad. Not only will holding your anger in result in a continuous buildup of stress in yourself, it will eventually diminish the bond of the relationship. Here are some possible solutions:

- Forgive (see chapter 3).

- Express your anger to a photo of the person, then forgive.

- Express your anger to a rock or a tree (they don't care, but they will listen) and then forgive.

These techniques will work, but only if you would rather be happy than be right. If the brief feeling of power you get from expressing your anger to a person whom you know will respond in kind is more important to you than the relationship, then I can't help you.

Bridging the Gap

Sometimes the stresses of life reach a point where physical tension dampens emotional responses and one or both people in a relationship begin to feel an ever-widening gap between them. When that happens, all the attractions that keep people together seem to fade. Men can become so involved in work, convincing themselves that they are doing it for their family, that they ignore their family and wonder why the marriage fails. Women can feel so abandoned by their spouse that they close down their feelings and seek other ways to relieve their stress. The only way out of this bind is for one person in the relationship to make the effort to bridge the gap. Admittedly, this isn't always easy.

When Gloria and I first went to Africa, we left an active life of graduate school, social activities, and employment. Our post was in Cotonou, Dahomey (Benin today), and our home was in a tiny village across the river from Cotonou. It's hard to describe what our new life was like to people who have never been there, but I'll give a few indications.

Having come from urban America, we abruptly found ourselves in a place where the language was different (French was the official language, of which I spoke a little and Gloria none); the food was different (goat was our main source of meat, although we occasionally got horse); bugs were rampant (I got malaria and we became indifferent to roaches); medical care was nearly nonexistent (I couldn't even figure out how to open a French ampoule of medicine); the average temperature was 95°F (35°C) and the average humidity 95 percent; and drums beat twenty-four hours a day from some source we never discovered. On top of that, I had to learn a job I wasn't prepared for and which sometimes took me away for weeks at a time, and Gloria was stuck at home with our two-year-old son and the houseboy, with no friends to talk to.

After six months, we were like strangers who lived under the same roof and shared the same bed, without any emotional contact and very little conversation. Gloria had no understanding of my work, and I had no concept of her sense of isolation, but I did know that the marriage was going downhill fast. I made the decision that I wanted this to change and took the initiative. First, we needed to communicate, and we had to have something to communicate about, so I began the journey back to love by borrowing news magazines from the US Embassy, reading them to Gloria in the evening, and practically forcing her to comment on the stories. Then I started playing chess and card games with her; I found someone to teach her French and hired her as my secretary to get her out of the house and among people. By that time more young Americans our age with the Peace Corps and the embassy came to live in the area, and a reasonable social life began.

I know that our situation was rather extreme, but it illustrates the fact that someone has to make changes when stress gets in the way of happiness. Even in the best of circumstances couples can lose contact with each other from the stresses of work and family life. When life gets too hectic for too long, I recommend making appointments with each other for fun time, and I mean actually scheduling it into your personal calendars. Some people think it ridiculous to schedule appointments with your spouse, but Gloria and I have done it on occasion because it works.

The whole problem of bridging the gap reminds me of Rupert Holmes's song "Escape," which is usually called "The Piña Colada Song." In it, a man is sitting in bed with his wife asleep next to him. He is reading the newspaper and thinking about the fact that the spark had gone out of their marriage. Then, in the "Personals" column he reads a letter from a woman looking for a man who likes Piña Coladas and "getting caught in the rain," among other things, and inviting the right man who reads the letter to escape with her to a new life. The man replies with a personal ad in the same paper saying that he, too, likes Piña Coladas and other things, and inviting the woman writer to meet him at a bar to plan their escape. Well, as he's waiting in the bar, in walks his wife, the writer of the first letter. They discover that neither of them knew the other liked Piña Coladas and the other things, so they plan their escape to a new life. It was a roundabout way to communicate, but it worked. At least in the song.

CHAPTER 9

Divorce

Sometimes marriages just don't last. It's a terrible thing, but it's a fact of modern life. However, divorce isn't as common as we've been led to believe. While it does appear that the United States has the highest divorce rate in the world, the commonly quoted statistic that 50 percent of all US marriages end in divorce is not only highly misleading, it isn't true. The latest statistics, which date from 2003, indicating a divorce rate of less than 40 percent are also misleading. Here is an important quote from an article by Dan Hurley in the *New York Times* dated April 19, 2005:

> Researchers say that this [statistic] is misleading, because the people who are divorcing in any given year are not the same as those who are marrying, and that the statistic is virtually useless in understanding divorce rates. In fact, they say, studies find that the divorce rate in the United States has never reached one in every two marriages, and new research suggests that, with rates now declining, it probably never will.

That's the good news. Unfortunately, divorces still happen too frequently, and the process is not only time-consuming and expensive, it often ends in bitterness between the former partners.

I don't have any quick-fix techniques to prevent a divorce, but perhaps knowing the common causes of divorce, and the common factors in a happy marriage, will help. Citing Russell and Susan Wild's book entitled *The Unofficial Guide to Getting a Divorce* (John Wiley and Sons, 2005), a Wikipedia article states that the common grounds for divorce are irreconcilable differences, incompatibility, long separation, adultery, cruelty, abandonment, mental illness, and criminal conviction. Another study by Jeffry H. Larson, chairman of the Brigham Young University Family and Marriage Therapy Program, divides the factors that contribute to an unhappy marriage and may lead to divorce into three categories. The first has to do with individual characteristics:

- Highly neurotic traits

- Anxiety

- Depression

- Impulsiveness

- Self-consciousness

- Vulnerability to stress

- Anger/hostility

- Dysfunctional beliefs

The second category involves what the professor calls "Couple Traits":

- Dissimilarity

- Short acquaintanceship

- Premarital sex (especially with many different partners)

- Premarital pregnancy

- Cohabitation
- Poor communication and conflict-resolution skills

The third category of disruptive factors involves the context of the marriage:

- Younger age
- Unhealthy family-of-origin experiences
- Parental divorce or chronic marital conflict
- Parental or friends' disapproval
- Pressure to marry
- Little education or career preparation

In contrast, Professor Larson lists the factors that will most likely produce a happy marriage:

- Individual traits:
  - High self-esteem
  - Flexibility
  - Assertiveness
  - Sociability
- Couple traits:
  - Similarity
  - Long acquaintanceship
  - Good communication skills
  - Good conflict-resolution skills

- Context:
  - Older age
  - Healthy family-of-origin experiences
  - Happy parental marriage
  - Parental and friends' approval
  - Significant education and career preparation

Remember that all these factors are only indicators, not absolutes. Just because you have anxiety, a short acquaintanceship, or parental disapproval doesn't automatically mean that your marriage will fail. What matters most is what you do to keep it alive and happy. "With effort and commitment and caring," says Larson, your marriage can be a happy one. "Just don't expect it to be easy," he adds.

A Secret Technique

There is a Hawaiian expression that describes a technique that will guarantee a happy marriage: *hau'oli ke kekahi, hau'oli ka hale*: "happy spouse, happy house." Like many good techniques, it's very simple, but not very easy.

What is simple is the concept: keep your spouse happy, and the marriage will be happy. It's the application that is hard, because what makes your spouse happy may not make you happy.

Some years ago, I had a woman client who could not communicate with her husband. He was so different from her in interests and disposition that they didn't connect. To help her get closer to her husband, I recommended a technique that involved her learning to walk like him and talk like him. After a month of this, she reported that her husband was warming up to her. But while he was being more friendly, conversing more, and apparently liking her more, at the same time she was discovering that she really didn't like him as a person. She did get what she wanted, but then she decided that she didn't want what she got.

The "secret technique" works perfectly, but only if you are willing to adapt. I'm not speaking of compromise, which in English implies giving up your principles to please someone else. That will never work well. But being willing to change some of your habits, attitudes, and behaviors is absolutely necessary to making your marriage work. Life as a single person is not at all the same as life as a married person, just as life with a roommate is not the same as life with a spouse—quite apart from the sexual side of it. As my wife says, "You've got to give up the *me* for the *we*."

I have to admit that sometimes it feels more like I'm giving up the *me* for the *you*, especially when I'm involved in a computer game and she wants me to take out the garbage, but those are little things that I can live with. What helps me adapt is that I have drastically reduced the number of things that I won't change, so that even though I might moan and grumble a bit at having to change a pattern of mine in favor of one of hers, it's almost always no big deal and I'll do it without resentment.

What helps Gloria adapt, on the other hand, is her willingness to tolerate a multitude of my idiosyncrasies and to change her pattern when she encounters one of my few rock-solid ones.

I read about another solution that was quite interesting. A man said that in his family he made the big decisions and his wife made the little ones. He decided who should be president, what to do about global warming, and how to handle international relations, and she decided where they should live, how to rear the children, and what kind of car to buy.

If you always want things your way, your priority is to exert your power, not to express your love. A marriage, under those circumstances, becomes a sham, an excuse to have a legal servant and concubine, male or female.

If you are interested in a happy marriage, you might find some inspiration in these definitions of the Hawaiian word for marriage, *ho'ao*, taken from the official marriage statement used for ceremonies in the Order of Huna International:

> Some idea of the meaning and intent of marriage can be had by noting these translations of the word *ao*: "to become enlightened; to take care of; to learn and to teach; to experience; a new shoot of taro (symbol of love); a team; a way of life; the *aumakua* (guardian spirit)." The word for "man" is *kane*, and the word for "woman" is *wahine*. The first can also be translated as the "breath of life" and the second as "the holder of life."

In fact, I think the rest of the statement might be helpful, too, because in addition to some original thoughts it

CHAPTER 9

contains an adaptation of an excerpt from Kahlil Gibran's *The Prophet*:

Aloha! We are gathered here to celebrate the union of this couple in marriage. It is a ceremony of commitment, and it is well to speak of the meaning of this commitment. First, I would speak of love, and have you know that it is more than just a feeling that appears on some occasions and disappears on others. Rather, it is like a stream that ever flows yet never flows away. It is the willing act of sharing your God-given life, of supporting one another in times of joy and sorrow, of cherishing, of helping one another to grow and blossom in fullness.

Ho'ao is the ancient Hawaiian word for marriage. The esteem in which marriage was held is indicated by the fact that the marriage ceremony always took place on the eleventh night of the old calendar, the night called *Huna*. Marriage is considered to be a commitment, yet not to each other. Marriage is not a state of mutual custody. Rather, it is a commitment to do certain things with and for each other. In this respect it follows the Hawaiian word for "commit," *ho'oko*: "to fulfill; to succeed; to give support; partnership; companion; strength."

True marriage, then, is a commitment to love, to fulfill your lives together. Let there be spaces in your togetherness, and let the winds of the heavens dance between you. Love one another, yet make not a bond of love. Let it rather be a moving sea between the shores

240

of your souls. Fill each other's cup, yet drink not always from the same cup. Give one another of your food, but eat not always from the same bowl. Sing and dance together and be joyous, yet let each one of you have your times alone, even as the strings of a guitar are alone, though they quiver with the same music. Give your hearts, yet not into each others' keeping, for only the hand of Life can contain your hearts.

And stand together, yet not too near together. For the mountains of the islands stand apart, and the koa tree and the palm grow not in each other's shadow. Yet both the mountains and the trees stand on the same ground and reach toward the same sky.

It is good, then, to remember the unique identity of your soul, while knowing you are one in spirit."

Following this beautiful passage is the Marriage Vow: "I commit myself to share my life with you, to cherish you, to support your success, to encourage your growth, and to increase your joy."

He pili kua, he pili alo: Back to back and face to face.
— Hawaiian proverb about marriage

Chapter 10

The Rest of the World

Relationships in general will be our focus now, including those that do not include parents, children, relatives, friends, lovers, or spouses. More techniques will be presented that can apply to all relationships.

MASTERS AND SLAVES

This life is such an interesting experience. We are all participants in a vast game that we all agreed to play before we got here. The game consists in trying to thread our way between two worlds, each with a different set of rules. On the one hand, we have this three-dimensional physical world wherein we have to find food, shelter, clothing, and companionship and to confront other game players struggling to comprehend and cope. On the other hand, we have—let us say—a four-dimensional world that shows this reality to be a product of our own minds, an illusion. From the fourth-dimensional point of view, this world we consider reality is actually a "dream-world."

What is the good of knowing all this? It depends on whether you want to be a slave of life or its master. To be a slave of life is to accept everything around you as the ultimate reality and to act as if you have no control over it. It is to identify with the waves of energy that pass through you from time to time, which we call emotions. It is to think that your emotions *are* you, that they are yours, and to let them condition your thinking, when in reality the energy has been colored by your thinking all along. It is to be like a puppy chasing its own tail.

Then there is the problem of other people. Everything would be great if only they all did what you wanted or expected them to do. But other people are such contrary beings. Often they would rather do what *they* want, rather than what we want, even when we "know" that ours is the best way. So when they don't act according to our expectations and desires, it upsets us terribly, causing emotional (energetic) trauma and feelings of helplessness and hopelessness. But—and consider this carefully—when others don't act according to our desires and expectations, then perhaps something is wrong with our desires and expectations and not with their behavior.

A slave of life is also terribly bound by material possessions such as money, land, and goods. Their loss or lack causes emotional trauma and feelings of hopelessness and helplessness, too. We seek such tangible objects out of a need for security, but what a fragile and ephemeral type of security it is! The biblical parable of the man who worked for years and years to fill his barns and granaries with riches, only to find on the very day he thought he had attained material security that he was to depart this life the same night, reflects a fundamental truth. We are only passing through this life. The material world is only a tool for our experience. We are bound to suffer if we try to base our security on swirling atoms held in a temporary pattern and to think of the pattern as the only reality.

The master of life—which every human being has the immediate potential to be—knows that three-dimensional experience is no more than a reflection of thought. As a master of life you realize that you choose what you experience through your basic beliefs. You realize further that to change your experience you have only to change your beliefs, and you understand the difference between desire and belief. You know that you, and only you, are completely responsible for your happiness or unhappiness. And you also understand one of the most important truths: that the way in which you experience life depends on how you choose to react to what happens to you. For this is an inborn, inalienable power that each of us has. We choose to be happy or sad, disgusted or overjoyed, impatient or understanding, bigoted or tolerant, inflexible or flowing. The slave chooses, too, but he lets the will or acts of others determine his choice, thus putting his power in their hands, and then he tries to blame others for his failure or unhappiness. The master of life chooses the way he wants to feel and to react in terms of what will be the most effective for him, regardless of what happens.

In the movie, *Matrix Revolutions*, I was extremely impressed with a short scene in which the human hero, Neo, fights a titanic, hand-to-hand battle with Mr. Smith, a humanoid computer program. Time after time, Mr. Smith beats Neo to the ground, and time after time, Neo gets back up to fight again. Finally, after one battle sequence in which Neo, apparently defeated, is on the ground again, Mr. Smith speaks to him, using Neo's birth name:

> Smith: Why, Mr. Anderson, why? Why, why do you do it? Why, why get up? Why keep fighting? Do you believe you're fighting for something, for more than your survival? Can you tell me what it is, do you even know? Is it freedom? Or truth? Perhaps peace? Could it be for love? Illusions, Mr. Anderson. Vagaries of perception. Temporary constructs of a feeble human intellect trying desperately to justify an existence that is without meaning or purpose. And all of them as artificial as the Matrix itself. Although, only a human mind could invent something as insipid as love. You must be able to see it, Mr. Anderson, you must know it by now! You can't win; it's pointless to keep fighting! Why, Mr. Anderson, why, why do you persist?
>
> Neo: (getting up once again): Because I choose to.

You are all, at all times, masters of your fate, insofar as your power to choose your reactions goes. The primary difference between the slave of life and the master of life is that the slave refuses to accept responsibility for his choices and so remains a slave, while the master of life chooses knowingly and is free.

People speak of the courage it takes to choose effectively and of the struggle to choose one reaction over another. Actually, the only courage involved is that of risking someone else's displeasure at your choice. And the only struggle is against your own fear and doubt. Of course, it is easier to float than to swim—easier to go with the flow than to direct your course—but floating may bring you up against sharp and unpleasant rocks, while swimming brings you to safety.

To continue the swimming analogy, let us conceive of a particular experience in life as a rip tide. A rip tide is a strong current running from the shore out to sea a hundred yards or more. Let's use it to represent a life experience over which you apparently have no control. Caught in the rip tide, a slave of life either panics and tries to struggle against the current, in which case he quickly loses strength and drowns, or he gives up all hope and floats out to sea with the current, in which case he drowns anyway. The master of life, however, flows with the current until he feels its power weakening, and then he swims around it and back to shore. Both slave and master undergo the same experience. The difference is in how they react to it. To master life is not to control it; it is to master your relationship to it. A master surfer does not control the wave. He masters the art of riding it.

PRINCIPLES OF LEADERSHIP

Leadership is a special kind of relationship that some people have with others. I have already mentioned that it is natural for human beings to form hierarchies for the purpose of accomplishing things. Depending on who is at the top and what his or her power-needs or love-needs are, what is basically natural can become either supernatural or unnatural.

To the military mind, leadership is just that: the ability to lead. When Dwight D. Eisenhower was the commanding general of Allied forces in Europe, he was said to have demonstrated the principle of leadership by placing a string on a table. First, he demonstrated bad leadership by pushing the string forward from the near end, which only resulted in a tangle. Then, to demonstrate proper leadership, he pulled the string forward from the far end, like a general leading his troops, and of course the string stayed nice and straight. Great demonstration! If only people were strings. (By the way, I have the greatest respect for a military that carries out a purpose of preserving peace and protecting the people, but it is interesting to note that generals were not the first ones to land on the beach at Normandy.)

Politicians view good leadership somewhat differently. As Abraham Lincoln put it, "Honest statesmanship is the wise employment of individual meannesses for the public good."

Tribal chiefs have yet another viewpoint. In the movie *The Emerald Forest*, when a tribal chief was asked why he didn't just tell his people what to do, he being the chief, he said, "You don't understand. I'm the chief because I tell them what they want to do."

My own ideas about leadership are based on the seven principles of Huna:

- The world is what you think it is. As the leader, you define reality.

- There are no limits. As the leader, you make the rules.

- Energy flows where attention goes. As the leader, you direct the focus.

- Now is the moment of power. As the leader, you energize the present moment.

- To love is to be happy with. As the leader, you support your group.

- All power comes from within. As the leader, you are the source of authority.

- Effectiveness is the measure of truth. As the leader, you make or approve the plans and modify them as needed.

And now, here is what I call the "ABCs of Leadership":

- **A**lways **B**e **C**onfident

- **D**ecide **E**ach **F**ocus

- **G**et **H**igh **I**nside

- **J**ust **K**eep **L**oving

- **M**ake **N**ew **O**pportunities

- **P**ractice **Q**uiet **R**esolve

- **S**eek **T**he **U**nique

- **V**alue **W**orldly (experience)

- Xpect (the best)
- Yield Zip (meaning "never give up")

What Do You Want?

I often meet people who tell me they don't know what they want, in terms of purpose, goals, or relationships. My experience in helping such people over the years, however, has taught me that everyone knows what they want. It's just that some people are afraid to express it because they might not get it, and then they would feel bad. Daring to express what you want, even if it is only to yourself, increases your personal power and self-esteem. Expressing what you want in a relationship can help to keep you out of a bad one, or help to heal an unhealthy one. First, though, you have to deal with the fear, and this Dynamind Technique is a wonderful resource for that:

1. Bring your fingertips together and take a deep breath.

2. Make a statement like, "When I think of saying what I want, I feel anxiety in my _____(body location), and that can change. I want that feeling to go away."

3. Tap your chest, the upper web of both hands, and the base of your neck seven times each. Bring your fingertips back together.

4. Take a *piko-piko* breath by inhaling with your attention above your head and exhaling with your attention below your feet.

5. Think of saying what you want again, and check how you feel. If necessary, repeat the process.

The Dynamind Technique can also be used to reinforce your ability to express what you want in a relationship. Here is how you might use it that way:

1. Hold your hands as in the exercise above.

2. Make the statement, "I have the power to choose what I want; I have the right to choose what I want; I have the desire to choose what I want; I choose what I want right now."

3. Tap as above.

4. Breathe as above.

Knowing or deciding what you want in any encounter is highly useful, because it helps you keep your focus on what's important and keeps you from getting distracted by nonessentials. When I am working with clients, I always keep in mind what I want, which is to help them solve a problem. In order to be more effective in achieving what I want, I always ask the client what he or she wants at the beginning of the session. This helps both of us avoid endless talking about the problem and enables us to get right to solving it.

When involved in healing a relationship of any kind, keeping in mind what you want the healing to accomplish will help avoid digressions into power plays, blame and complaints, and criticisms. Then you can move toward the healing with more clarity.

Chapter 10

Reconciliation

What do you do when you have broken up with or become estranged from someone you care about? From time to time people ask me to bring a spouse or a lover or friend back into their life after that person has left in anger or chosen to be with someone else. On occasion, when I probe for motivations for the reconciliation, the client will say something like, "So that he/she will crawl at my feet and beg for forgiveness!" Well, that's a client out the door. That kind of desire for "reconciliation" is nothing but a desire for power and punishment, and it's no wonder that the person's partner left. Reconciliation can only occur when both people have a good reason for getting back together.

Ongoing feelings of hurt and anger can interfere even with good motivations, however, so here is a technique that has often proven successful:

The Play-Ball Technique

The Play-Ball Technique is within the category of passive telepathy, which is the act of broadcasting a mental message in such a way that the intended recipient has the free will to respond to it or not. Although this technique is good for helping to reconcile friends, lovers, and spouses, it is also good for reconciling disagreements between parents and children, customers and clerks, or citizens and bureaucrats.

1. Imagine that you and the person with whom you want to reconcile are standing in an open field.

2. Imagine that you have a ball of some kind, and start a game of tossing the ball back and forth.

3. Continue until the game is enjoyable and you feel better about the other person.

I have to tell you, sometimes this technique is easy and sometimes it is hard. When I played ball with my father after he died, it seemed like he was trying to cause me injury rather than play ball. After a while of doing my best to avoid getting hit, I changed my framework, reinterpreting his action to see it as a challenge. Soon afterward, we had fun together, and I felt that our relationship was healed in a way it needed to be. Of course, the whole thing was symbolic of my feelings about my father and not necessarily of his feelings about me.

The following excerpt from my novel *Dangerous Journeys*, describes two other examples of this technique, both taken from real-life situations. The scene begins after the hero, Keoki, has just alienated a new acquaintance:

By this time Keoki had stopped beating himself for being so rude and was trying to find a way to heal the situation. A plain apology would no doubt be politely accepted by Jeff, but it wouldn't improve their relationship. An abject apology would probably be received as a mockery. What could he do that would work? What would Gramps have done?

Thinking of Gramps brought up a time when he was getting into a series of fights with another kid in grade school. He hadn't wanted to fight any more, but he couldn't think of any way to stop without breaking the other guy's arms and legs. One evening Gramps had helped him to imagine that he was playing catch with his enemy. At the beginning of the imagination, he and the other boy kept trying to bean each other with a baseball, but by the time Keoki finished some five minutes later he was imagining that they were tossing the ball back and forth in a friendly way. In school the next day the boy glared at him, but didn't try to start anything. Within a couple of days he even stopped glaring at Keoki. Within a couple of weeks they were playing football on the same team without any fuss. Keoki never became friends with the boy, but neither were they enemies any longer.

What the heck, thought Keoki. What kind of ball do Britishers play? He thought of cricket, but he really didn't know much about the game. He knew they played rugby, but he also knew that it was a rough sport and that didn't seem appropriate. They also played soccer, he remembered. He would try that. In his mind he set up a soccer field where he and Jeff could practice. It took some effort to imagine Jeffrey in a soccer outfit, but he finally managed it. The next problem was that Jeff wouldn't play. Keoki would kick the ball to him, gently, and Jeff would simply fold his arms and look the other way. Keoki was stumped for a couple of minutes. Then he got the idea to turn the soccer ball into a globe of the earth. That got the imaginary Jeff's attention, and with a little exertion of will Keoki was able to get the ball going back and forth quite nicely. When his image of Jeff started to smile, Keoki figured it was enough for the time being.

Relationships with Events

Some of the most difficult kinds of events with which we have to relate are war, disaster, and death.

Why does war exist? People engage in war because they want to love or be loved. Although this idea may sound absurd, let's give it a closer look, because if we can understand the motivation for war then we might be able to redirect it.

The most fundamental human need is to be accepted—that is, *loved*—and the most fundamental fear is to be rejected. The old idea that survival comes first doesn't hold up in the light of experience, because it doesn't account for those who risk their lives for others—even strangers—and for those who commit suicide. And the fear of death is the fear of the ultimate rejection: by life itself.

Acceptance can be sought from oneself, one's environment (including people), or one's God, and many different strategies exist to ensure acceptance. If these strategies are pursued without fear or fear-based anger, the result will be peace and cooperation. But as the fear of rejection increases, so does the tendency to seek acceptance by control or submission. The result is emotional repression, social suppression, and the use of violence to prove one's power or to make others accept oneself whether they want to or not.

In the case of war, the leaders who make the major decisions, motivated by their standards of self-acceptance or acceptance from their group, set the criteria by which to judge the "other side's" behavior as acceptable or unacceptable, And those who obey the orders to march off to death and destruction are motivated by the desire to be accepted by doing the "right thing," or by the fear of being rejected and/or punished for not doing it. What's so sad is that their fundamental intention is so good.

There is no glory in death and destruction. The so-called glory of war lies in the experience it offers of incredible bravery, intense companionship, demonstrations of skill, overcoming of limitations, successful protection of one's country or loved ones, and adulation for the winners. Yet, until we find a better way to satisfy the need for acceptance from our group and the desire for real power, people will continue to go to war out of love.

Our great challenge, therefore, is not just to end war; it is also to develop alternatives that still provide the benefits that only intense experiences can generate as well as satisfy the need for love.

A Response to Tragedy

When a great tragedy occurs, people with any degree of compassion naturally want to help. If we are on the site, we can plunge in with our minds and hearts and hands, like rescue workers, medical personnel, and blood donors do. If we are not on-site, we can donate money to helping organizations like the Red Cross and others, or we can pray for the victims and their friends and families. Still, none of this seems like enough, and a sense of helplessness can move many people to feelings of anger and retribution, or fear and confusion.

Let us give our desire to help a clear and effective focus. In addition to whatever else you feel is appropriate, let's give our prayers, energy, light, love, journeys, and any other distant healing we can use to support the helpers, healers, and peacemakers in the area of the tragedy who are working to assist those in pain and to resolve the problems. Especially whenever we feel helpless about a situation, let us bless and strengthen their spirits and actions. Here are some specific suggestions for what to do each time you think of the situation and its aftermath:

1. Pray to a Higher Power to help the helpers (who include the healers and peacemakers).

2. Imagine the helpers being surrounded by healing light and/or being assisted by angels or other spirit helpers.

3. If you know how, do an inner symbolic journey to help the helpers.

4. To the best of your ability, bring your own spirit to a state of peace by meditating on the beauty and goodness in the world, and practice positive expectation that, no matter what happens, the work of the helpers will be successful, in this world or another. This may be the most difficult of all to do—and the most beneficial.

CHAPTER 10

LIFE, DEATH, AND HUNA

Throughout the ages, philosophers, scientists, theologians, and anyone else who has paused to think about the whys and wherefores of things have wondered about the experience and meaning of life and death.

The Absurdists have decided that life and death are meaningless, so the best thing to do is to ignore death until it happens. The Resisters see life as good and death as bad; they do everything they can to prolong life and avoid death without regard to the quality of life or the desire for death. The Beyonders say that life is a proving ground; if you follow the rules you'll have a different and better life after death, but if you break the rules you'll have a different and worse life after death. The Cyclists hold that the essence of a person experiences life and death over and over again until, by grace, individual effort, or gradual evolution, there is no need for either one.

Of course, given human creativity, there are many variations and alternatives to the above. Here is one derived from the principles of Huna:

First, life and death exist as experiences. The one who decides their meaning and consequences is *you*, based either on what someone has taught you or on your own conclusions. No matter what life and death may actually be, your beliefs about them will govern your related thoughts and actions.

Second, Huna assumes that existence is infinite and that therefore life and death and time and space are just names for different types of experience.

Third, a belief is simply a way of organizing your perceptions or expectations to allow yourself certain experiences and disallow others. By reorganizing your perceptions and expectations about life and death, you can change your experience of them.

Fourth, all experience is happening now. Time is merely a belief. To people of the past, right now you are unborn; to those of the future, you are already dead.

Fifth, life and death are part of the impulse toward fulfillment that we call love. Love changes the lover and the beloved, and without change there is no existence.

Sixth, the power of life and death comes from within. Not from within the personality or the body, but from our infinite spiritual source. "Outside" factors may influence the timing and manner of life and death, but they do not cause the experience.

Seventh, regardless of what anyone says about life and death, what really matters is what you think. You have the right to choose any set of ideas or beliefs about life and death that makes sense to you and helps you deal with those experiences.

YOUR RELATIONSHIP WITH THE WORLD

Recently I was taking a morning walk through a familiar neighborhood, beside a familiar golf course, along a familiar coastline, and past familiar trees and flowers to a familiar cliff overlooking the ocean. My Body was giving me the sensory input of sights, sounds, smells, and feelings, while my Mind was registering patterns and making interpretations.

"That's a street, that's a path, that's a tree, that's grass, that's a cloud, that's the ocean . . ." said my Body.

"Ho hum, here's the same old walk again," said my Mind. "Borrring!"

Then my Spirit interrupted. "Wait a minute! Look again. That leaf wasn't there yesterday. Those clouds and those waves are not the same ones, either. And did you ever notice that particular ridge outlined in that particular way by the sun? Look again. Today is different."

Suddenly I realized, in a very real and physical way, that my Spirit was right. It was not only a different day, it was, by any meaningful definition of reality, a whole new world. It only seemed the same because I was looking at it through old eyes.

One very useful characteristic of human beings is our ability to recognize patterns and to apply pattern recognition to our environment in thousands of practical ways.

In the natural environment, we can learn weather patterns that will help us prepare for planting or hunting or sheltering, animal and plant patterns that will assist in our food gathering and production, rock and land and water and star patterns that will help us on our journeys. I have used such patterns on numerous occasions throughout my life for such things as finding my way through the Sahara Desert, navigating across open stretches of ocean, and getting in and out of wilderness areas on Kauai.

In an urban environment, we can learn street and traffic patterns to help us go where we want to go, building and address patterns to help us find what we want to find, and people patterns to help us define who is doing what and why. In my travels around the world, I have encountered people wearing many different kinds of costumes whom I was still able to acknowledge as policemen because of pattern recognition. This same ability has enabled me to drive a car in various countries, even when it was necessary to vary the pattern for driving on the left or the right.

We can recognize a forest, regardless of the types of trees in it. We can recognize dogs and cats, regardless of the specific breeds. We are really, really good at recognizing patterns.

However, pattern recognition presents a serious problem when we stop looking at the world as it is and begin looking at the patterns instead. When we stop looking at people and look only at patterns of people, we can fall easily into the traps of racism, prejudice, bias, and bigotry. When we stop looking at our environment and look only at patterns that we superimpose on it, we lose touch with the power and healing and adventure and awesome variety that actually exists. And when we stop looking at ourselves and look instead only at some perceived pattern of ourselves, we tend to identify with the pattern and become afraid of change.

Perhaps this is the key to the age-old idea that most people are asleep and that a true perception of reality requires that they somehow wake up. If so, they aren't really asleep at all. They are just looking at the world through old patterns, old eyes. The solution, then, is not to wake up; it is to perceive differently. Not everyone wants to do that, but if you do, here is a suggestion:

1. Try looking at a familiar environment and finding something new in it. To begin with, "look" with any of your senses for something you've never noticed before, or use a sense that you've never used in a particular way for a particular thing in that environment, like experiencing how differently a breeze feels on various parts of your body.

2. As a variation, when you enter a new environment, purposely look up, down, and in the corners for details you might normally gloss over. With practice, you'll be able to sense your world differently more often. And if you forget, as I still do from time to time, trust that Spirit will remind you.

3. Finally, if you are truly interested in learning to see differently, it's a good idea to study just enough science and metaphysics to understand that the universe is changing constantly, even while it keeps repeating patterns. *Which means that the patterns are always changing, too.* There is power in that knowledge, and if you love life enough you can find it by putting your old eyes aside and using new ones.

Yesterday was, and never will be again.
Tomorrow isn't, and can't be reached.
Today neither was nor will be.
Today is different.

Index

A

abandonment, 24–25
Absurdists, 258
abuse
  emotional, 189–91
  physical, 186–89
  sexual, 191–92
  verbal, 186
acceptance, 255
acting, 120–22
adenosine triphosphate
  (ATP), 153
adequacy, 62–63
admiration, 43
adolescent, 180
affirmation, 43
aggression, passive, 12
aloha, 214
Aloha International, 263
analysis, 117–19

anger
  power and, 12
  in relationship, 224,
    229–31
anticipation, 44
appreciation, 43
approval, 10, 133
attraction
  emotional, 213–15
  mental, 215–16
  sexual, 208–10
'Aumakua (higher self), 168
auras, 166–67, 214
authority, 127
  figures, 182
awareness
  of body, 75–78
  of hearing, 89–92
  information and, 81–82
  of movement, 78–81

water, 153

weeds, 138

When I Say No I Feel Guilty (Smith), 197, 198

Wild, Russell and Susan, 234–35

women, differences from men, 7–8

world, relationship with, 259–62

About the Author

Serge Kahili King, PhD, has been trained in Hawaiian shamanism, African shamanism, international management, and psychology. He is the founder of Aloha International, a worldwide network of people dedicated to making the world a better place through promoting Hawaiian culture, spreading the Aloha Spirit, and teaching and healing with the ancient knowledge of Huna, a Polynesian philosophy of life.

He and his wife, Gloria King, have been married for fifty-two years, and they have three children and eight grand-children. Serge and Gloria live on the island of Kauai,

Hawaii, and assist other members of Aloha International in operating a Hawaiian museum, teaching Huna, teaching hula, teaching Hawaiian string figures to children, teaching Hawaiian history and culture, and supporting Hawaiian cultural events. Serge also travels the world presenting workshops on Huna and healing and spends his spare time writing books.

For more information on the activities and resources of Aloha International, visit www.huna.org, www.huna.net and www.alohainternational.org, or email huna@huna.org.